Ions, Edmund
Against behavioural-
ism

DATE DUE

OCT 14 '97			

The Library Store   #47-0103

Against Behaviouralism

Against Behaviouralism

A Critique of Behavioural Science

Edmund Ions

ROWMAN AND LITTLEFIELD
TOTOWA, NEW JERSEY

First published in the United States in 1977
by Rowman and Littlefield, Totowa, N.J.

© *Basil Blackwell 1977*

British Library Cataloguing in Publication Data

Ions, Edmund
    Against behaviouralism.
    1. Social sciences
    I. Title
    300'.1   H61

    ISBN 0–87471–864–3

Printed in Great Britain

Contents

The scale scores and demographic variables were correlated with each other and the correlation matrix (with squared multiple correlational coefficients in the principal diagonal) was analysed into two factors, determined by their eigenvalues exceeding unity. The principal component method of factor analysis was used and the factors were orthogonally rotated by the normal varimax criterion. . . . The scales were administered to 46 persons who were attending a ten day Quaker-UNESCO seminar on Grindstone Island in the summer of 1967. . . .

We conclude that militarism is at least partly a function of hypercritically restrictive childhood training which produces a 'love affair' between anal personality traits and authoritarian military ideologies. . . .

Article on 'Militarism, Personality and other Social Attitudes':
Journal of Conflict Resolution XIII (No. 2) 1969, pp. 210–19.

Thus in mid-Han times there came to be a pseudo-science of history which had an immense vogue for several centuries. . . . A number of purblind thinkers set to work to classify all abnormal phenomena, ranging from comets to women growing beards, and to link these with the moral judgements on record. An extensive literature grew up, of which only a small part has survived, for the good sense of the Chinese people came to revolt against the plain absurdities of it.

E. R. Hughes, *Religion in China* (London, 1950) p. 53.

Introduction

The role of the behavioural scientist in modern society is comparable to that of the astrologer in earlier times. The comparison may seem otiose, but let it be reviewed. In his study of religion and the decline of magic in England Mr. Keith Thomas provides a detailed treatment of astrologers in the late sixteenth and early seventeenth centuries.[1] They performed a variety of functions, but chief among these was the business of prediction. They predicted and advised on matters ranging from marriage and personal relationships to business forecasts, market movements, social and political matters, even on medical and psychological problems. Their advice was sought by kings, courtiers, the gentry, and by the common people, who digested their forecasts in almanacs which had the appearance, even if they did not contain the substance, of scientific credibility.

It was customary for many of their predictions to be hedged about with 'ifs' and 'buts' or other caveats, or to be phrased ambiguously so that if things went wrong, the astrologer's reputation was not impaired. As for the claims of astrology and of its practitioners, Mr. Keith Thomas tellls us:

1. Keith Thomas, *Religion and the Decline of Magic: Studies in Popular Beliefs in Sixteenth and Seventeenth Century England* (London, 1971), pp. 286 ff.

Nothing did more to make [it] seductive than the ambitious scale of its intellectual pretensions. It offered a systematic scheme of explanation for all the vagaries of human and natural behaviour, and there was in principle no question which it could not answer.[2]

The parallel with behavioural science today is not inexact. Against this it may be argued that the behavioural sciences have been prime instruments in despatching just that mixture of mystification and superstition peddled by the astrologers, and that this was secured by requiring beliefs to submit to tests of evidence. This is true, and the behavioural sciences can take much of the credit for throwing light in dark corners. What is also true, however, is that they have become bolder in their claims and pretensions. They investigate and seek to explain all kinds and conditions of social phenomena, subjecting older disciplines to what are claimed to be more rigorous forms of inquiry. Historical studies, jurisprudence, the study of politics, anthropology and linguistics are increasingly taken to come within the purview of behavioural science, along with more familiar candidates, such as psychology and social psychology.

The chief weapons in this form of intellectual imperialism are quantification and computation, assisted by statistical theory and method. Since there is no end to the things we can quantify in modern society, behavioural science has become a new heavy industry, absorbing immense resources, both capital and human, on both sides of the Atlantic. The result is a sort of cultural Moloch feeding on mountains of data served up by zealous scholars and armies of research assistants. Numeracy sometimes appears to be at the cost of literacy. The effects of this at the level of culture seem to me profoundly disturbing and ultimately – if paradoxically – anti-social.

This is not to say that the investigation of social phenomena by sophisticated statistical methods is not an important undertaking. I have little sympathy with the Luddite mentality which regards the computer as the work of

2. *Ibid.*, p. 324.

the devil. Computers have their uses and abuses. In astronomy, for instance, the calculations required for plotting stellar transits, or again in medicine, especially epidemiology, the computer's ability to store and retrieve immense amounts of data is a sufficient retort to Luddite prejudice.

The argument begins when we quantify, then process and interpret the human act. In this respect, behavioural science represents a form of collectivism which runs parallel to other developments in this century. However high-minded the intention, the result is depersonalisation, the effects of which can be felt at the level of the individual human being, and not simply at the level of culture. My concern at these developments prompts the present study.

Behavioural science is now a house of many mansions, characterised by its methods more than by its subject matter, and since it reaches into so many disciplines, separate or cognate, this imposes on the essays that follow a particular form. I have thought it best, for clarity of exposition, to devote separate essays to distinctive fields of enquiry, but I intend them as chapters within a single framework on a common theme. The work of some scholars, past and present, clearly qualifies them for discussion under the rubric of behavioural science – B. F. Skinner, for instance, or J. von Neumann and the new generation of game theorists in what are called the 'policy sciences' in some quarters. Other candidates may seem more surprising – Noam Chomsky, for instance, and Lévi-Strauss. But I trust the argument within the particular essays show why I locate the work of these distinctive and distinguished scholars within the corpus of behavioural science as this has developed in recent years.

In a work of this nature one's intellectual debts are likely to be more long standing, or more subterranean, than can be stated or even recognised. One clear debt is to Isaiah Berlin. Anyone who had the good fortune, as a graduate student, to join the Berlin seminars on social and political theory knows not only the unique excitement he generates in ideas, but also his ability to convey that explanation – historical, social, or philosophical – takes many forms, and that this is one potent answer to materialist or determinist theories of history or of the social process.

Another debt is to the late Edward Evans-Pritchard. In moments of flight from the rarefied atmosphere of Nuffield College, I was fortunate to be brought into Evans-Pritchard's company ('E.P.' as he was affectionately known to a coterie) at informal lunchtime gatherings. From these and other encounters came the realisation, however inadequate, that the western mind bears many encrustations of time and place. The best tribute I can pay to Evans-Pritchard's memory is to say that I think I begin to see why, at the end, he returned to his first passion – history.

Other debts are more immediate. I thank colleagues in the science departments at York University for discussing points relating to recent developments in the sciences. At the History Department, Professor Gordon Leff, whose prodigious range embraces medieval thought and the epistemology of the social sciences, made valuable criticisms of a first draft. Dr. Bryan Wilson of All Souls College also made pertinent and constructive criticisms. Needless to say, I remain entirely responsible for deficiencies that remain. At the Institute of Social and Economic Research, York, Professor Jack Wiseman provided a quiet refuge in the early stages of gestation. Miss Barbara Dodds and the assistant secretaries typed up various drafts with astonishing speed and skill. At the Morrell Library, the librarians dealt patiently with too many requests, and allowed me to pillage various sections of the library for extended periods.

I had hoped to complete this critique one or two years ago, and appreciate the patience of friends and colleagues who have inquired about its progress. Delay was caused by a three-year spell with the editorial staff of *The Economist* for part of each week, whilst continuing to teach on the remaining days at York. Stepping outside the academy in this fashion was salutary in every possible way, since it provided fresh perspectives and the interlude was valuable for thinking. through one or two aspects of the discussion contained here.

I owe the title of this study to Sir Isaiah Berlin, who bequeathed it after a lecture he gave at York a few years ago. My former teacher inquired about work in hand and I indicated what I was about. I also confessed that I could not think of a suitable title. 'Against Behaviouralism', said the sage instantly. 'You are against dogma.' The suggested title stayed in the mind and I doubt that I could improve on it, in the letter or the spirit.

E. S. I. *York, 1977*

I

Abstractionists

Bertrand Russell's definition of mathematics as 'the subject in which we never know what we are talking about, nor whether what we are saying is true'[1]* has the air of an impish epigram yet it contains profound elements of truth. It also reflects the range and capacity of one who knew the strengths but also the limitations of his subject. Another of Russell's observations deserves attention:

> When actual objects are counted . ∴ . or when, in any other way, mathematical reasoning is applied to what exists, the reasoning employed has a form not dependent upon the objects to which it is applied being just those objects that they are, but only upon their having certain general properties.[2]

In other words, when we quantify what we take to be individual characteristics of persons, groups, or things, it is not the *individual* characteristics we quantify, but examples of general properties which we presume inhere within our selected instances. So our problems are by no means over when we quantify: indeed, they are merely beginning. We quantify in order to measure differences. Heisenberg's discovery that the simple act of measurement can have

---

* All notes are to be found at the end of the relevant chapter.

substantial effects on the thing measured was in its original context confined to quantum mechanics, but is now a commonplace in the world of science. The implications of Heisenberg's discovery have yet to be accommodated within the methods of behavioural science, even though they apply here with peculiar force, most obviously because of the human element.

It follows that the more prolific the measurements in any piece of behavioural research, the greater the number of possible distortions built into the research design. This discomforting paradox is not presented in the typical manual on behavioural science techniques.

More discomfort awaits us when we return to the controversies within mathematics. Quantitative methods in behavioural science assume, *inter alia*, formalised procedures on agreed sets of axioms, rules of inference, and transformation rules. There is no such agreement among mathematicians. One has only to turn to the debate on Boolean algebra, or later debates on Peano's axioms, or in our own time Gödel's paper, disposing of the consistency theory and presenting new possibilities for alternative truths which cannot be demonstrated within an existing calculus.[3] The mathematics deployed by behavioural scientists must therefore be regarded as sets of blunt instruments, adequate for the crudities of ordinary discussion and investigation, but lacking the elegance, the beauty and the mystery of mathematics.

Social scientists may reasonably protest that although the higher mysteries of mathematics are not featured in their explorations, nevertheless the low-level calculations of social science do have the virtues of consistency, order, and objectivity, which is after all the main *raison d'être* for mathematical and statistical notation in the behavioural sciences. We ought therefore to conduct the argument at a utilitarian, not at a metaphysical level. Let us concede this, for the moment, and merely note in passing that every calculation in behavioural science – whether it features simple arithmetical addition, or matrix algebra, rests ultimately on metaphysical postulates which await solution and universal agreement.

Mathematical and statistical excursions in behavioural science commonly involve comparisons of magnitude. Magnitude expresses magnitude: nothing less, and nothing more. The *explanation* of a particular magnitude, or of a series or collection of magnitudes, is a logically discrete activity from the expression of it or them. As Hempel noted, endorsing Russell, mathematics may be valuable, even indispensable as an instrument for the expression of certain types of knowledge, but it does not contribute anything to the content of our knowledge on empirical matters.[4]

If mathematics is no more than a useful set of ancillary heuristics, therefore, it cannot and should not be an end in itself in the behavioural sciences. In the work of most social scientists mathematics is kept in its proper place. Nevertheless, it would be possible to compile a formidable list of publications where the writer clearly takes his primary task to be solving one or more of a series of equations, rather than to discuss the topic in hand.[5]

The application of mathematics to social investigation cannot of itself furnish 'proof' of what is the case now, or what may be the case in future. At most it helps to indicate greater or lesser degrees of reliability in tests of evidence. On the vexed question of the predictive value of generalisations, behavioural science never establishes what *will* occur, since to do so entails proving the general proposition that the future will resemble the past, unless the particular instance under discussion is first demonstrated to form a single class, on agreed criteria. At best a certain order of probability is suggested, yet probability theory is itself a minefield of speculative metaphysics, so that here again, the behavioural scientist necessarily lowers his sights and takes as given what are still matters of deep controversy.[6]

Attempts to seek out general laws, or to establish law-like generalisations covering all sorts and conditions of human circumstances have proved fruitless, and even the search for theories of the middle range has so far proved unproductive.

Nevertheless, the search for low-level generalisations continues, with the earlier quest for law-like generalisations decently obscured and re-named multivariate analysis, where the task is to seek out correlations of higher and lower degree.

Multivariate analysis requires at all stages mathematical notation. The essentially static and inflexible nature of mathematical notation for exploring dynamic social processes is best discussed in terms of some familar techniques of behavioural science. The most obvious one is the selection of variables for the purpose of investigating correlations in factor analysis. The term 'variable' is a misleading one, since although its allotted numerical magnitude may fluctuate during an investigation, the 'variable' retains its initially defined notation throughout. It varies, that is to say, only in terms of an expressed magnitude.

The implications of this can be more serious than is commonly allowed, since the allocation, or the arrogation, of a particular magnitude to a changing social circumstance is a bold and contentious step which could be the subject of dispute at every stage. In the initial selection of variables, it is common practice to regard some as 'key' or independent, others as dependent. This again is a necessary simplification, since *in social processes* 'variables' are necessarily *inter-*dependent and therefore, in the strict sense of the word, dependent, not independent. Failure to discover the degree of inter-dependence is not in itself an argument for ignoring it. Hidden variables are ignored because they are not perceived.[7]

'Independent' and 'dependent' variables are thus arbitrary distinctions, based not on any scientific or mathematical theorem or a deductive argument, but on a combination of subjective hunch, personal estimating, and intuitive evaluations. Once selected and allocated, the variables circumscribe and condition the content of the inquiry. Replication of the inquiry for purposes of checking is extremely rare. Where it is possible, or attempted, it assumes closed systems and constant conditions. Neither assumption is justified by ordinary experience.

The device of rank ordering, and the use of interval and ordinal scales for factor analysis carry further presumptions into the inquiry. For particular stages of the investigation, rank orders are held constant: variation, promotion, or demotion within the rank order is not possible, since this would require a fresh research design. Ordinal scales are assumed to be mutually exclusive, whilst interval scales assume that the intervals between any two pairs of adjacent classes are equal. In modal investigation, it is assumed that the most frequently observed quality or characteristic is the dominant, or the most significant one, though the proof of this in any particular investigation cannot be derived merely from frequency distribution. Here, as elsewhere, statistical techniques provide tools for measuring observed frequency, but not 'significance' in the customary meaning of the term.

Another minor abuse of language is involved in what are termed 'tests of significance'. These are applied at various crucial stages of the analysis, and have the function of some magical incantation to allow the analysis to proceed to further flights of abstraction. But in themselves, tests of significance are fairly arbitrary, based on convention rather than mathematical theory, and may vary from 1 per cent to 5 per cent depending on the inquiry and the conventions adopted.[8] Why the upper limit of the zone should be around 5 per cent is not self evident and is not firmly established by theory: like the selection of variables, it is a subjective and fairly arbitrary process imported on the basis of general criteria, rather than the particular grounds of the inquiry in hand, which of course cannot supply them.

A conclusion of null hypothesis on the basis of statistical tests is another arbitrary procedure, the subject of controversy among mathematicians, since null hypothesis depends not merely on the number of tests, but also on the number and the nature of the hypotheses tested. In recent years the whole question of statistical inference has been the subject of sharp debate among specialists, but the controversies have not stirred the waters of ordinary social science research. Instead, there has been a tendency to sidestep controversy in the search for what are claimed to be new levels of sophistication in the investigation of behavioural phenomena.

A good example of this is Lazarsfeld's general mathematical model for what he terms 'latent structure analysis', building on the work of Guttman and Mosteller.[9] The general purpose of the model is to go beyond manifest, or extrinsic variables to what are termed 'latent' or intervening variables. But an initial postulate of the model requires that responses be formulated in dichotomous terms, and a related postulate of the basic model is that answers to dichotomous questions may be assigned plus or minus signs in order to build up 'response patterns', with relative frequencies. These in turn stimulate more data for mathematical treatment. What the model fails to provide is any rationale of its initial postulate, that meaningful responses may be derived from dichotomous propositions, or the arbitrary allocation of plus and minus signs to given responses. Binary thinking is useful as a stage post in making distinctions for the purpose of separating out the many ingredients which go to make up the individual's world view. As a prime tool of inquiry, however, or as an intellectual disposition, it falsifies *ab initio* the very nature of the social phenomena it purports to explain.

Notes to Chapter I

1. Bertrand Russell, 'Mathematics and the Metaphysician', – reprinted in Russell, *Mysticism and Logic and Other Essays* (London, 1917, new ed. 1963), pp. 59–60.
2. Bertrand Russell, *The Principles of Mathematics* (2nd ed. London, 1937) xvii.
3. Cf. Ernest Nagel and James R. Newman, *Gödel's Proof* (London, 1959), esp. pp. 66, 85 ff. Although Gödel addressed his arguments to his fellow mathematicians, it applies with even greater force to the more recalcitrant fields of social investigation. Gödel argues that even where formal languages

exist, they can state a variety of truths which are not deducible from the axioms of the given system. In other words, several different explanations can be derived from the same data, no explanation necessarily precludes another, or an alternative explanation, and none is self-evidently, or even inherently better, or more fruitful, or even more 'accurate' than another, until 'accuracy' is defined by agreed criteria.

4. Carl Hempel, 'On the Nature of Mathematical Truth'. Hempel's paper first appeared in the *American Mathematical Monthly*, Vol. 52 (1945), but has been republished in various collections since then. And see Russell, *Principles of Mathematics*, Chap. XIX, 'The Meaning of Magnitude'.

5. In the vast literature which has issued from the behavioural sciences it may seem invidious to select any particular specialisation, but Econometricians would be strong candidates for leading the field, closely followed by new varieties of behavioural scientists. In the United States, jurimetrics (the statistical investigation of judicial decisions), international relations, political science of the Yale/Michigan 'Behavioralist' persuasion, are each producing an extensive literature which belongs to mathematics before it belongs to the traditional disciplines on which it is based.

6. Probability theory goes back to Pascal and Fermat in the seventeenth century, but Laplace (*Traité de Probabilité*, Paris, 1886) is the usual 'modern' starting point. A good introduction to the problem from mathematical perspectives is A. Kolmogoroff, *Foundations of Probability* (transl., New York, 1950; original ed., Berlin 1933). The work of Carnap, *Logical Foundations of Probability* (Chicago, 1950) and R. von Mises, *Probability, Statistics and Truth* (New York, 1939) are familiar texts, but see also H. E. Kyberg, *Probability and the Logic of Rational Belief*, (Middletown, Conn., 1961), E. Parzen, *Modern Probability Theory and its Applications* (New York, 1960), and L. Breiman, *Probability and Stochastic Processes* (Boston, 1969).

One should note that the elements of probability theory are based on coin-tossing experiments (Bernouilli trials) where trials are independent of each other and sequential, and normally allow only two possible outcomes for each trial so that the order of probability remains the same. The resulting set follows a binomial distribution within a well defined sample space. Yet few if any of these factors are present or available for the typical research design affecting *social* phenomena, even when algebraic notation is used in order to suggest transition probabilities (Markov chains) in order to construct stochastic matrices. (See also p. 23, p. 33 fn 1, *infra*.)

7. Cf. F. J. Belinfante, *A Survey of Hidden-Variable Theories* (Oxford, Pergamon Press, 1973). Belinfante's survey applies more strictly to discussions in natural philosophy, but his monograph is replete with lessons for behavioural scientists.

8. Cf. E. Caulcott, *Significance Tests* (London, 1973) Chap. 5, pp. 66 ff.; J. K. Backhouse, *Statistics: an Introduction to Tests of Significance* (London, 1967); Denton E. Morrison and Ramon E. Henkel (eds.), *The Significance Test Controversy* (London, 1970), especially W. W. Rozeboom's article, pp. 216–30, and Parts IV and V, pp. 283–311.

9. Paul Lazarsfeld and Neil Henry, *Latent Structure Analysis* (Boston, 1968), Chaps. 1 and 2.

II
Inductivists

In their formative period, the social sciences admired and attempted to copy the methods of the physical sciences in the search for generalisations of universal application. The admiration persists, and shows itself in ambitious attempts to gather immense quantities of data, presumably on the primitive belief that there is safety in numbers, and should some of the data prove unreliable, then sins of omission or commission may gain absolution or remission in the law of large numbers.

One of the ironies of this situation is that it is based on a view of science and scientific experiment that is essentially nineteenth-century, and at least a hundred years out of date. In the most fruitful areas of discovery in modern science, such as molecular biology and biochemistry, the concern is not with broad generalisations, but with exciting particularities: not with aggregation, but with uniqueness. The structure of a single cell or the universe contained in a minute drop of amino-acid contains the keys to discovery at the frontiers of biochemistry. In physics, too, it is the individual particle that excites most attention, not aggregations of assorted matter, though attempts are of course made to reach certain universal conditional statements.

The aggregations of the behavioural sciences, therefore, contrast sharply with the particularities of the biological and physical sciences, to the extent that they passed each other

going in the opposite direction some time ago. There is a
further moral for behavioural scientists who claim that direct
observation is the touchstone of any rigorous inquiry. One of
the most important discoveries in physics in the last quarter
century is the omega minus particle. But the existence of
omega minus was inferred long before it was observed.
Intuition, not observation, was the key to discovery. Indeed,
on any strict criteria it still exists as a construct, rather than a
directly observed actuality. And whereas behavioural science
assumes that social roles, attitudes or opinions may be
separated into distinct categories for analysis, we may draw
another moral from modern quantum theory, that an
electron can be a particle and a wave at one and the same
time. Mutually exclusive categories are no longer the
paradigm case, and classification itself is not a central
purpose.

On the broader canvas of scientific method, Popper's
rejection of induction-based logic, and his argument that
scientific advance proceeds by refutation, has important
implications for the fact-gathering expeditions of behavioural science. Popper has his critics, but his rejection
of induction-based logic came after a thorough grounding in
mathematics and physics. If the witness of a practising
scientist is preferred, P. B. Medawar provides it in eloquent
and witty style in his 1968 Jayne lectures.[1]

Medawar does not go so far as Popper in an outright
rejection of induction, but he is highly critical of the view that
scientific thinking proceeds by tidy logical argument.
Methodologists without experience of scientific research
seem unaware, Medawar states, that 'nearly all scientific
research leads nowhere – or, if it does lead somewhere, then
not in the direction it started off with.'[2] Medawar adds his
own estimate that 'about four-fifths' of his time has been
wasted, leading nowhere, and making no contribution to
science. He further believes that this is the common
experience of people who are 'not merely playing follow-my-
leader in research.'[3]

Medawar perhaps stretches the point somewhat, since the

mental processes he describes as wasted effort – four-fifths of
his time in all – would surely include the perception of
negative leads which, though not productive in any formal
sense, are ultimately productive in the sense of helping to
redirect thinking to more productive areas of inquiry.

But this is to quibble. Medawar's main point is that there
are highly subjective elements in scientific inquiry, that
successful inquiry proceeds by way of intuition, hunch,
insight, flair, imagination, and even luck. He further argues
that in choosing between the importance of mere observation
and data gathering on the one hand, and these other, non-
logical, unscripted techniques on the other, the latter are of
much greater importance and value for furthering scientific
inquiry at every level – from day-to-day work, to major
discoveries in science.[4] Indeed, Medawar adds, those who
believe that the ritual of fact-finding and the mumbo-jumbo
of inductive procedures make up the 'scientific' element in
scientific research have got the priorities exactly reversed. The
generative creative act is of much greater import for advances
in science than tabulation or data collection.

These reflections of a scientist can be placed against the
injunctions of behavioural scientists who argue that value-
free objectivity is the touchstone of scientific inquiry and
advance. Medawar's arguments are the more persuasive in
that they arrive from experience within scientific research,
rather than from presumptions drawn from outside the
scientific community. Nor can Medawar be accused of
adopting an appealing or fashionable 'Two Cultures' attempt
to bridge the world of science and of the humanities. His
devastating attacks elsewhere on the mistiness and obscurities
of Teilhard de Chardin's thinking, and to a less pointed
degree on Arthur Koestler's theories on the act of creation
(where Medawar argues cogently that Koestler shows no
adequate grasp of the importance of criticism in science),
acquit him of such a charge.[5]

Elsewhere, Medawar has reminded us that we possess no
logical machinery for evoking hypotheses, and he takes up
Whewell's point that one should always make a sharp

distinction between facts and observing facts: that facts cannot be observed *as facts*, but are interpreted by us, by means of inherited information. Without venturing into the abyss of the epistemological controversy on the one hand, or the mind/body problem on the other, we can agree with Medawar that perception involves several concurrent processes, and that among these are some form or forms of internal circuitry which involve some type of feedback mechanism, wherever this may be located. This brings us back to induction, but Medawar neither fears nor avoids the charge. For him, science is an imaginative search guided by preconceptions, based on personal, critical judgments. 'Science is not classification; it is not a search for laws. Biology has far fewer "facts" than sociology.'[6]

Some points raised in the last chapter on mathematical reasoning may be linked here with points on scientific method. In science, mathematics can display, or suggest, connections between scientific statements, but cannot prove the truth of those statements. However close the mathematical 'fit' between one set of data and another, whether expressed as a high-order correlation, or as a statement of probability – the statement remains a hypothesis about, rather than the proof of, any assertion about the data.[7]

To the extent, then, that behavioural science pursues a supposed value-free objectivity by the application of mathematical techniques to data, it departs from scientific method as it is accepted and practised in the physical and natural sciencies. This is not to say that the collection of data is not a valuable exercise. One can no more generalise about the virtues of data collection than one can generalise about collecting bric-à-brac. At certain times and in certain places it is useful for particular purposes: elsewhere its virtue is not self-evident, even though it might have a function, or functions, of sorts. The danger is that data collection sometimes becomes an end in itself, and it is the data which generate the hypotheses, rather than the hypotheses which proceed to the relevant data for their investigation. Obviously, only the most obtuse social scientist would amass

data without some idea of its utility or purpose, but clear
purpose can become obscured by the immense corpus of data
available in modern society, so that the variables taken to
relate to a particular question or problem become those
which are self-evidently quantifiable. Thus the test of
acceptability for a potential variable is whether it is
immediately quantifiable, not whether it is of strategic, or
latent (however defined) importance. But these tendencies
and their implications are best discussed in more concrete
terms in succeeding chapters.

Notes to Chapter II

1. Reprinted under the title *Induction and Intuition in Scientific Thought* (London, 1969).
2. *Ibid.*, p. 31.
3. *Ibid.*, p. 32.
4. *Ibid.*, pp. 43–4.
5. See Medawar's essays on *The Art of the Soluble* (London, 1967), which include Medawar's review of Koestler's *The Act of Creation.*
6. Sir Peter Medawar, 'What is Scientific Method?' – in *Discovery & Design* (BBC, London, 4 September 1967).
7. For a more extended discussion on this point, see Sir Harold Jeffrey's *Scientific Inference* (2nd ed., Cambridge U.P., 1957), esp. Chap. 1, 'Logic and Scientific Inference'. The perspectives are those of the Plumian Professor of Astronomy and Experimental Philosophy at Cambridge; credentials acceptable, one trusts, to behavioural scientists.

III
Generalists

The founding fathers of social science are not to be blamed for some retrospective burdens wished upon their early hopes by modern system builders. Comte has suffered in this regard, particularly when he is credited with the search for discoverable general laws relating to society. A more meticulous *scrutin de texte* than is commonly given in modern sociological texts and commentaries discloses that Comte made a number of important qualifications, easily over-looked and even suppressed in the rush to quantify. In his hierarchy of the sciences, rising from astronomy at the base to sociology at the apex, Comte was careful to note that the hierarchy was marked by the law of increasing complexity and decreasing generality. He further stressed that sociology differed from the other sciences in its necessary reliance on the historical method 'which investigates not by comparison, but by gradual filiation'. Here, as elsewhere, Comte stressed that sociological inquiry without historical investigation and analysis is useless.[1]

Comte also drew a careful distinction between the sociological and the mathematical point of view, arguing indeed that mathematics had no place in sociological studies proper. He distinguished further between the study of society as a collective, and the study of pluralities of individuals. Thus, when the Belgian statistician Adolphe Quetelet sought to bring his mathematical theory of a normal curve of distribution for social phenomena – with its related phenomenon, 'the average man' – within the purview of 'social physics', Comte labelled Quetelet a metaphysician and promptly renamed his own system 'sociology', to distinguish it from social physics and a spurious scientism. Empiricists of some modern schools of sociological analysis, with their batteries of scales, rank orders, Lorenz curves, and an armoury of statistical techniques, are thus the heirs of Quetelet, not of Comte.

Pareto has suffered a fate similar to that of Comte. Few thinkers in the tradition of sociological thought had a clearer notion of the extreme limitations of social science, both as an activity and as an intellectual discipline. No doubt Pareto's early training as an engineer alerted him to the folly of seeking easy analogues between building bridges and constructing a science of society. Like Hume, Pareto not only observed meticulously, but kept continually in mind the essential point that observed regularities are not in themselves evidence of a causal nexus; and that there is no necessary connection between experimental uniformities, or correlations, and their antecedent events. In his discussion on 'Sociology as a Science' Pareto stressed that in the study of society a hypothesis may imply the existence of certain facts, but those facts may lend themselves to many alternative hypotheses.[2] Even in economic behaviour, which Pareto regarded as more hospitable to mathematical study, he cautioned:

> The simplest thing one can say in economics is that the economic equilibrium results from the conflict between tastes and obstacles; but the simplicity is only apparent, since one then has to go on and take account of an intricate variety of tastes and obstacles. The complications in sociology are greater still . . .[3]

Comte's distrust of mathematics and Pareto's cautions (together with Pareto's extended discussion of four different categories of non-logical action in the first volume of the

Treatise on General Sociology) have clearly found little echo in the quantitative schools of behavioural science which grew up in the United States between the 1930s and the 1950s. As we will go on to note, some of the excesses of those years are now largely overtaken by an increased concern with what is termed 'qualitative' analysis – though whether the new concerns turn out to be little more than semantic window-dressing must also be discussed. We ought first, however, to give one or two examples of the type of quantitative work we are criticising.

In 1949 George Kingsley Zipf published the fruits of labours which had occupied himself and his assistants at Harvard for something like twenty-five years.[4] Zipf claimed to have discovered a principle of universal application for all human beings and all societies. This was the 'principle of least effort' – which holds that individuals and societies act so as to minimise the expected, or the probable average rate of work. Zipf drew his data from an immensely wide range of sources: demographic and economic; technical and scientific; semantic and literary. The theory has been criticised briefly by Kenneth Arrow,[5] but the grounds of his critique are technical – namely that the theory:

> does not constitute a properly developed mathematical model. The fundamental postulates are nowhere stated explicitly; though mathematical symbols and formulas are sprinkled rather freely through a long work, the derivations involved are chiefly figures of speech and analogies, rather than true mathematical deductions . . .

Arrow's critique, therefore, is of the lack of mathematical rigour. The implication seems to be that if Zipf had got his equations right, he might have proved his theory, or at the very least, done a great deal better, though Arrow does not supply any positive evidence for this in his brief remarks. He suggests that Zipf's model 'is certainly rational', but the criteria of rationality are not discussed.

An alternative approach to Zipf's theory is to ask whether it stands the tests of ordinary experience. It is simply not the case that at all times and in all places individuals and societies act so as to minimise the expected average rate of work. The most obvious individual example is the creative artist: Michelangelo on his back beneath the ceiling of the Sistine Chapel, or his six years painting the Last Judgment. But other examples are too numerous to mention. The sculptor, the composer, the craftsman, the scholar – indeed all who find some satisfaction in their work for its own sake – as distinct from monetary reward – falsify Zipf's theory. Traced to its presuppositions, Zipf's theory turns out to be the philosophy of entrepreneurial capitalism in its crudest form. At the time he wrote (the late 1940s), Zipf and his assistants might well have felt that the rest of the world was following the United States in the drive for economic efficiency and maximum growth by cutting labour costs and other overheads. In the 1970s, debates on the quality of life and limits to growth make these assumptions very debatable.

Zipf's failure to provide a general social theory did not inhibit attempts elsewhere to base such a theory on quantification. In a series of essays and articles during the 1950s Herbert A. Simon sought to formulate 'a consistent body of theory of the rational and non-rational aspects of human behaviour in a social setting'.[6] The 16 essays gathered in his *Models of Man* are characterised by more sophisticated mathematical techniques than those used by Zipf. But the prior simplifications – in the interests of model building – are no less startling. In a paper on *Bandwaggon and Underdog Effects of Election Predictions* Simon's first simplifying assumption is that (V), the percentage of voters who actually vote for a candidate A, in a two-candidate election, depends on two factors: these are (i) the percentage who intended to vote for A prior to the publication of the prediction, and (ii) the prediction itself – that is (P) – the percentage who, according to the prediction, intended to vote for candidate A in any case. This abstract formulation, anaesthetised from the uncertainties of politics, allows the argument to proceed to graphical demonstration (the graphs containing the two functions (V) and (P)). There follows Simon's bold claim that he has 'shown that it is always possible *in principle* to make a public prediction that will be confirmed by the event'. Simon adds, 'This proof refutes allegations commonly made about the impossibility, in principle, of correct prediction of social behaviour.'[7]

Pollsters will wish that it were so. They will also wish that successful forecasting might be built on the deployment of two tautologies, namely that the results in a two-candidate election depend upon (i) the percentage voting for the winning candidate exceeding that for the losing candidate; (ii) a prediction of the winning percentage proving to be correct. Simon's 'model' of political behaviour turns out to be no more than an exercise in *a priori* analytics.

One further essay in the collection may be examined, since the work deals with group interaction, and the approach adopted by Simon is common to some other explorations of group theory. In 'A Formal Theory of Interaction in Social Groups',[8] Simon postulates that a social group – by which he means simply 'a group of persons' – may be characterised by four variables, all functions of time. These are: (I) Intensity of *interaction* [author's italics] among the members; (F) the level of *friendliness* among the members; (A) the amount of *activity* carried on by members within the group, (E) the amount of activity imposed on the group by the external environment.

Simon's principal aim is to discover an equilibrium position for the group, that is, where it has stability and is least likely to fractionate. A related interest is to discover the conditions under which groups dissolve. He concedes that the units in which his selected variables can be measured 'are somewhat arbitrary' – which in turn allows him to use only the ordinal properties of the measuring scales and of certain 'natural' zero points. Other assumptions are built into the model, including an 'appropriate' (nowhere defined) level of interaction for levels of friendliness.

It is perhaps unnecessary to mention that Simon's analysis is algebraic, though the equations are heavily interlarded with provisos on the 'roughness of the empirical observations', and similar phrases. The question that arises, however, is in what sense Simon's observations may be taken as 'empirical', as claimed, since they are not drawn from any empirical data, but in fact amount to no more than Simon's subjective, abstracted assumptions of how groups behave, and what effect increased, or decreased interaction has upon the group. Interaction is not specifically defined, and this is not surprising, since it would require a discussion infinitely longer than that afforded by Simon's short paper. But consider further the assumptions built in to the model. Simon obligingly sets them out:[9]

(*1*) 'The intensity of interaction depends upon, and increases with, the level of friendliness and the amount of activity carried on within the group.'

Two hypotheses are thus present. The principal hypothesis is close to a tautology: intensity of interaction depends upon the amount of interaction, though intensity is not defined. The second hypothesis present is extremely dubious, since friendliness and cohesion are just as likely to result from respect for other persons' privacy as from an excess of interaction. Indeed, intensity of interaction may just as easily be an indicator of hostility. Feuding neighbours separated by a fence might well interact more frequently and volubly than neighbours on excellent terms who respect each other's privacy.[10]

Simon's further postulates may be mentioned without comment, since the same points apply.

(*2*) 'If a group of persons with little friendliness are induced to interact a great deal, the friendliness will grow; if a group with a great deal of friendliness interact seldom, the friendliness will weaken.'

(*3*) 'The amount of activity carried on by the group will tend to increase if the actual level of friendliness is higher than that "appropriate" [undefined) to the existing amount of activity, and if the amount of activity imposed externally on the group is higher than the existing amount of activity.'

Throughout Simon's essays, the initial hypotheses and postulates are no more than preliminary gestures – mere sign language to introduce mathematical theorising – not all of it elegant. If analysis and discussion in mathematical forms were intended to be contributions to pure theory, and in no sense recommendations for policy formulation or application, few objections could be raised. They could be regarded as a form of harmless intellectual activity, appealing to the theorisers, injuring no one, perhaps mentally stimulating for some.

It is clear, however, that Simon feels his speculations are suited to policy formulation and application, rather than mere exercises in abstraction. At several points in his essays, Simon suggests that his mathematical models can be applied to, for instance, administrative decision taking, servo-mechanisms in production control, and to social situations where conflicts of loyalties operate between groups. I can find no evidence that Simon's speculations have ever been applied, but this would be welcome since it would be at the very least intriguing to discover what results have flowed from them.

Although a generalist in the thrust of his interests, Simon's main preoccupation was with group theory. A scholar who cast his bread on much broader waters was Nicholas Rashevsky – who had a deep influence on his pupil Herbert Simon, at the University of Chicago, as Simon records in the Foreword to his Essays.

Rashevsky's *magnum opus* aimed at providing a 'biology of social phenomena', in the form of a sociology of conflict and war at the level of whole populations and societies.[11] His work resembles Simon's in the initial formulation of simplifying assumptions. Thus populations contain one – and only one – set of 'active' individuals; one – and only one – set of 'passive' individuals. Hence societies in conflict with each other are engaged in conflict between the 'actives' – that is, the élites – of each society. The length of conflict is dependent on the rate of destruction of members of the population. If the rate of destruction among the élite exceeds that for the 'passive' population, then the 'active' group can no longer influence the 'passive' group or persuade them to fight. Morale then breaks down and the capacity to fight ends. The side in which morale breaks down first loses the conflict.

Despite a sophisticated array of variables, ranging from areas of land to rates of retreat, Rashevsky's general theory adds up to a tautology. It states that when a nation at war loses its morale, when effective leadership no longer exists and when its forces are routed, it loses the war. One does not have to be a statistician, nor even a historian, to conclude that it could hardly be otherwise. Rashevsky's researches provide a useful curtain-raiser, however, for the army of statistical experts who have dominated the general field of conflict research and some aspects of defence studies and strategic thinking in the United States from the early 1950s to the present. Their influence has also been marked in the study of international relations, where a congruent development has been the building up of data banks for international, and more recently for 'cross-national' and comparative research across cultures and nations. But the literature spawned in these fields under what was originally termed 'the behavioural revolution' in political studies is now so vast that they must be treated separately in a later chapter.[12]

Notes to Chapter III

1. *The Positive Philosophy of Auguste Comte* (transl. Harriet Martineau), (3 vols., London 1913–15): III: Chap. XIII, pp. 383–4.
2. Vilfredo Pareto, *The Mind and Society: A Treatise on General Sociology.* (4 vols., 1963 Dover Publications edn.); IV, s. 2406.
3. Ibid., § 2408.
4. George Kingsley Zipf, *Human Behavior and the Principle of Least Effort* (Boston, 1949, repr. New York and London, 1965).
5. In Daniel Lerner and H. Lasswell (eds.), *The Policy Sciences* (Stanford, 1965), p. 149.
6. Herbert A. Simon, *Models of Man, Social and Rational: Mathematical Essays on Rational Human Behavior in a Social Setting* (New York, 1957), p. vii.

7. *Ibid.*, p. 86.
8. *Ibid.*, pp. 99–114.
9. *Ibid.*, p. 101.
10. Simon's theory and its postulates are neatly summed-up in the title of a once popular American magazine – *McCalls*, 'The Magazine of Togetherness'.
11. N. Rashevsky, *Mathematical Theory and Human Relations* (Bloomington, 1947) and Rashevsky, *Mathematical Biology of Social Behavior* (Chicago, 1951).
12. See Chap. VIII, below, pp. 76 ff.

IV
Empiricists

During the 1950s and 1960s most American sociologists prudently set their sights considerably below the levels of generality sought by Zipf, Simon and Rashevsky. They could be termed cautious empiricists, and they and their successors have come to be as wary of claims to prediction as they are of claims to uncover general laws. At most, probability statements are asserted, the strength or weakness of the probability varying with different cases and instances. 'Stochastic processes' is the favoured term to cover this flight to the refuge of probability statements, but there is a studied reluctance to express final or concluding degrees of probability in mathematical terms once the investigation is completed. This contrasts with the readiness to deploy the calculus of probability elsewhere in the analysis – from the initial selection of variables and parameters to the free use of stochastic processes within the analysis.[1] The reluctance to cast final results in precise or even recognisable statements of probability is thus selective and preferential. On closer inspection, the term 'probability' turns out to be much closer to 'possibility' – and earlier claims to precision evaporate in the conclusions.

Other devices are built into the investigation in order to excuse imprecision. They include standard deviation, standard error, 'confidence levels', 'normal distribution' and significance tests. These are derived from the analysis of aggregates, and from statistical theory, not from the observation of individuals or *human* groups, and whilst this may seem an obvious, even a trivial point, the implications for empirical research and conclusions (as distinct from theoretical abstractions) are far from trivial.

It may be objected at this point that most forms of social investigation do not take flight into the calculus of probability; that in most cases little more than summation is involved, or percentile grading, using simple vectors and matrices. But let us consider other aspects of the typical research design. Categorisation and classification are the first and least dispensable instruments of inquiry. The aim must be to reduce the number of possible categories within which observed instances are assumed to fall, so that they become manageable. No general rules are available for forming categories. Their selection is very largely an arbitrary, personal procedure, with a good deal of ad-hocery to make up for an absence of general rules or guiding principles. Categories may be factual, descriptive, or evaluative, ranging from a person's income, to the description of an institution as 'educational' (or not), to the expression of political values such as 'liberty', 'equality' or 'freedom'. The form and content of the analysis do not allow indiscriminate admixtures of the factual, the descriptive and the evaluative, however much ordinary experience confirms that they inter-penetrate, and that their true relationships can only be grasped within the context of that inter-penetration.

The familiar reply to this is that the process of separating, or factoring out is merely heuristic – a necessary stage for comparison and analysis. Some affinity with the methods of the natural sciences is usually invoked at this point. The underlying argument is that since this process has proved so successful in the natural sciences, it is therefore, *mutatis mutandis*, appropriate for the study of human societies.

Where categories refer to facts, as in a great deal of demographic and economic data – age, place of birth, size of dwelling, level of income, for instance – the parallel is apt. Where categories refer to description, it is less assured. Which institutions, for instance, can be categorised as 'educational'? Schools? Yes, surely. Libraries? Only partly – since they also provide entertainment. Television? The answer is uncertain, and must be hedged about with several qualifications on content, time and place. Where categories refer to evaluative or qualitative judgements, categorisation is even more hazardous. Equally, where responses are sought which invite respondents to give reasons for opinions held, or for courses of action, or merely invite them to express beliefs, then attempts to slot those opinions/beliefs/judgements into pre-selected categories essentially falsifies them by stripping them of the caveats and qualifications familiar in ordinary conversation and discourse. Again, there are social, non-physical categories which are arrived at by evaluation (Popper's 'social wholes') rather than by empirical methods or by experience.

The usual reply to these points is that the investigator takes care to formulate his categories only after a process of general inquiry; of asking around the subject among randomly selected individuals, and of getting the general 'feel' of popular attitudes and beliefs on the subject of the inquiry. But for objectivity, a prior step is surely required. By some non-subjective means the investigator must first discover whether, and if so to what degree his own opinions and judgements correspond to an average, or even a common point of view, so that his perspectives in formulating questions, and beyond these, categories of response, are not unduly biased. Few people – and fewer social scientists – are ready to concede that their views on all, or even some, subjects are those of the average man. If they do, then they delude themselves since the 'average man' is an abstraction; a figment drawn from aggregation.[2]

There is thus an insoluble dilemma *if* the chief claim of the investigator is that subjective views and personal idio-syncrasies have been reduced to a minimum in designing the research. The modern tendency is to admit that subjective elements are bound to be present, but that within these constraints, the research design proceeds in an objective fashion. But we are back to special pleading, since a central criterion of sociological investigation is that objective or detached estimations are to be preferred to purely subjective ones. Therefore it would be for an uncommitted observer, having no part in the particular inquiry, and not for the chief investigator, or designer of the inquiry, to assess whether the categories selected, and the scaled responses within those categories, faithfully reflect the perspectives of those contained within the sample.

Once more, it may be useful to take concrete examples from well-known studies. In a detailed investigation of the *American Soldier* in the 1940s, Samuel Stouffer and associates investigated, *inter alia*, 'the typical and general determinants of behaviour in the immediate combat situation'.[3] The investigators drew up a list of twelve factors held to contribute to stress, and six which help to offset stress. In the combat situation, as they phrase it, 'A tired, cold, muddy rifleman goes forward with the bitter dryness of fear in his mouth into the mortar burst and machine-gun fire of a determined enemy.' In this situation, Stouffer and associates argue (that is, they assume), that twelve stress factors are present, whilst six factors tidily (for statistical purposes) offset stress. Stress factors include 1. 'Threats to life and limb and health'. 2. 'Physical discomfort'. 3. 'Deprivation of sexual and concomitant social satisfactions'. 4. 'Conflict of Values'. 5. 'Lack of privacy', etc. Factors which offset stress include 1. 'Coercive formal authority' [listed first]. 2. 'Prayer and personal philosophies'. 3. 'Convictions about the war and the enemy', etc.[4]

A number of problems arise in interpreting these hypotheses. No statistical reason is supplied for the ratio of twelve stress factors against six factors reducing stress. They could in principle be in reverse ratio. Indeed, it would not be difficult to list only two or three stress factors, as against twenty or thirty factors off-setting stress. Secondly, if 'conflict of values' produces stress, it is difficult to see how 'convictions about the war' are countervailing in opposition, since they would seem either to cancel each other out, or, in concert, to add cumulatively to stress by inducing uncertainty and indecision. Again, it is not self-evident that 'coercive formal authority' off-sets stress, any more than that 'lack of privacy' (another word for companionship in arms) contributes to stress. Stouffer's lists are therefore not merely arbitrary; they are composed of false antitheses.

This major study of soldiers' attitudes has been acclaimed by social scientists for a quarter of a century now. It is taken as a model of sophisticated investigation in a commentary by Paul Lazarsfeld and Allen Barton in a more recent study.[5] They accept the inventory as 'typical and general determinants of behaviour in the immediate combat situation'. This is not, presumably, meant to imply that the typical soldier will have all, or even most, of these eighteen mental factors present in his mind when under fire. One may even doubt that he will have any of them in mind at that particular moment, in which case the usefulness of the inventory becomes questionable. Less conjectural is the simple fact that since the inventories were not composed or obtained under the actual conditions reported, they are thus recollections – more or less gathered in tranquillity – and as such are uncertain guides to on-the-spot reactions. Examined more closely, they turn out to be mere constructions placed upon past circumstance by a process of invention in a non-combat (and presumably non-combative) situation diametrically opposite to the conditions reported: in other words the inquiry was formulated as the responses were received, in unwarlike conditions. It is therefore difficult to see how the results of the inquiry meet the first prerequisite of scientific inquiry – that it should be in accordance with the observed facts.

Admiration for the Stouffer study has crossed the Atlantic. In his study *The Philosophy of the Social Sciences* (1970), p. 33, Mr. Alan Ryan praises Stouffer's work at one remove by citing the encomiums of Professor Lazarsfeld. Mr. Ryan suggests that studies such as *The American Soldier* expose our ignorance: they show to be false 'what we all know already,' by means of our subjective prejudices. The particular point at issue in

Mr. Ryan's commentary (p. 33) is the supposed disproof in
The American Soldier of the popular assumption that the
Negro soldier is, or was in general less ambitious than his
white comrades. But if Mr. Ryan had read *The American Soldier*
with his customary acuteness, he would have discovered that
Stouffer and associates (a) provide no convincing evidence
that there was indeed a genuinely popular assumption that
Negro soldiers lacked ambition, and (b) provide no
convincing proof of the opposite hypothesis, namely, that
Negroes are (or were, in World War II) more ambitious than
was popularly supposed. Stouffer merely established that
when a selection of Negro soldiers was questioned about the
possibilities of promotion, some declared an interest in
promotion. Those not questioned did not. No general
conclusions can be drawn from such a partial survey.

Another work much praised on both sides of the Atlantic is
the voluminous exploration of *The Authoritarian Personality*, by
T. W. Adorno and associates.[6] The title of the work is
misleading, since it is more precisely a study of anti-semitism
and social discrimination. This may not be the fault of the
authors, since publishers have been known to suggest eye-
catching titles. But *The Authoritarian Personality* resembles *The
American Soldier* in many respects. It is very long, very detailed
and crammed with data. Given present limitations of space,
the best course again seems to be to examine the most salient
aspects of the hypotheses in the work, and the methods used
for validating them.

The authors point out at the beginning of their study that
their 'major concern was with the potentially fascistic
individual – one whose structure is such as to render him
particularly susceptible to anti-democratic propaganda.'
They go on to anticipate the obvious question, why not give
equal attention to the 'potential antifascist'? They reply that
they do, in fact, study trends in opposition to fascism, 'but we
do not conceive that they constitute any single pattern'.
Whether this (subjective) view stands as a necessary, or a
sufficient argument for ignoring it, and whether there is
not what could be defined as a pattern of opposition for

the purposes of sociological investigation is not discussed.[7]

In developing their monocular approach to a complex phenomenon the authors and their assistants devised three main scales, the A–S (or anti-semitic) scale, the E (or ethnocentric) scale, and the F (or fascist/fascistic scale). Various sub-scales and different forms of the major scales are introduced. The inter-correlations among scales and sub-scales occupy much of the book. The A–S (anti-semitism) scale was constructed from fifty-two anti-semitic assertions, unrelieved by any assertion favourable to, or even neutral towards Jews.[8] Whether, and to what extent, the inclusion of pro-Jewish, or neutral sentiments or assertions about other religious or minority groups – or about injustice and persecution – might have produced different 'scores' among respondents, is not discussed. Since the purpose of the investigation was to identify and analyse those with extremist views, respondents were allowed to give answers to extremist viewpoints only. In other words, the prejudiced were *not* allowed to show any absence of prejudice; the less prejudiced were given no positive opportunity to display absence of prejudice, and the 'unprejudiced' were given no positive opportunity to display prejudice on topics other than anti-semitism.[9]

In the E, or Ethnocentrism scale, the thirty-four items are again entirely hostile to the groups in question. Twelve items contain specifically anti-Negro statements; the remainder relate to the dangers of diluting white, native-born Americanism with foreign admixtures. Jews are nowhere mentioned, on the stated ground that for the E scale, the emphasis is on ethnic group, rather than on race. For this study, therefore, Jews are classified as a race, Negroes as an ethnic group. The reasons offered for the distinction are as arbitrary as they are unconvincing.[10]

The construction of the F or Fascism scale was derived partly from the A–S and E scales, together with results drawn from Thematic Apperception tests carried out at the University of California on personality traits in relation to war, morale and ideology. One guiding hypothesis (of breath-taking ethnocentricity) was that fascism is 'most characteristically a middle-class phenomenon' – that it is 'in the culture' – and hence that 'those who conform the most to this [middle-class] culture will, therefore, be the most prejudiced'.[11]

In accepting the view that fascism is essentially a middle-class phenomenon, one wonders how much history the authors had read, though it might be a bold (middle-class) social scientist who would argue that historically, the appeal of fascism has been directed to, and gained its essential power from the working class and/or the economically deprived. If 'middle-class' means anything, it means educational advantage, and thus a better capacity for weighing, sceptically, extremist doctrines and ideologies. If economic and social deprivation mean anything, they mean lack of education, and thus, by a perfectly natural process, receptivity to extremist doctrines. The most cursory reading of history shows that fascist leaders do not come to power by reading papers to philosophical societies. Their audiences and their following are primarily among the deprived, even though they might take care to lull, or if possible, woo the middle classes.[12]

This brief digression is necessary because a considerable edifice within *The Authoritarian Personality* is built on the assumption that conformity with middle-class values is consonant with incipient fascism. Extreme conformism is equated with extreme prejudice and fascistic impulses. The more devoutly middle-class the respondent, it would seem, the more prejudiced he or she is likely to be. Scholarly naïveté rarely reaches such dizzy heights.

The significance of the formulation of the F scale becomes apparent when further details of the sampling methods used in the study are scrutinised. These are also given in the *Introduction*. The sample of 2,099 was drawn, as the authors admit, 'almost exclusively from the middle socio-economic class' (p. 22). It was also geographically confined. The great majority were Californians from the San Francisco Bay area. More than half were students – either full time or part time –

at universities or colleges. The bulk of the sample was made up of younger people. The authors assert that 'the findings of the study may be expected to hold fairly well for non-Jewish, white, native-born, middle-class Americans'.[13] One would add to this, 'young, Californian, college-educated' in order to define the sample more accurately. The authors follow up their implied generalisation with others, combining presumptuousness with face-saving clauses. 'When sections of the population not sampled in the present study are made the subjects for research, it is to be expected that most of the relationships reported in the following chapters will still hold – and that additional ones will be found.'[14] No supporting argument or evidence for this judgement are supplied.

One could go on at considerable length to discuss the ethnocentric hypotheses; the monocular scales and their effects on individual respondents and the inducements (3 dollars per session for 'clinical' sessions with subjects). But if the extreme crudities built into the initial formulation and design of the investigation are allowed to pass, it makes little sense to proceed to discussion and comparison of correlations and factor analysis, where distinctions are made to two decimal places among sub-sets, even when N is often of the order of 20, 10 or less, and where the ordinal differences between sub-sets are close to unity or zero.[15]

One could also go on to examine other ambitious exercises of the Stouffer/Adorno genre. In the era of the foundation award, where batteries of research assistants correlate positively with batteries of scaled responses in the research design, further examples are not lacking from a burgeoning literature. The difference between those of the 1960s and 1970s, and those of the 1940s and early 1950s, is that a technical armoury has been developed, where the initial crudities of the research design are masked by the deployment of an arsenal of mathematical devices. Chi squares; the Lorenz curve; the Gini Index; the Schutz coefficient; Kendall's Tau; Markov chains; Spearman Rank Order Coefficients – these are names to conjure with. They fit appropriately into different forms of inquiry in matrix algebra, graph theory and topology. But they have no formal correspondence with the quotidian of personal and social circumstance, and of the constant mutations between them.

This criticism applies to behavioural science much more than to empirical sociology, which has shown a healthy capacity to learn from the mistakes of past over-optimism. Although the search for greater rigour and mathematical sophistication has proceeded apace, the quest for general or overarching theory is now a thing of the past. We are unlikely to see ambitious projects in the style of Zipf or Rashevsky. Talcott Parsons has not been disposed to reply to his critics over the years, but if the search for a general theory of action goes on, its lineaments are locked in the mind of the master. In the late 1950s R. K. Merton's call for the exploration of theories of the middle range seemed a happy compromise between grand theory and micro-analysis, as well as inviting a convergence of general theory and empirical research. But in the decade and a half which followed Merton's call, the precise nature and content of such proposed theories cannot be said to have emerged, and the pessimism Dahrendorf expressed in his important paper *Out of Utopia* has been justified by the paucity of discovery.[16]

Western sociology seems now to have entered an introspective stage in which the old obsessions with methodology are being displaced by more fundamental questions on the philosophy and epistemology of sociology.[17] If this results in some paradigm shift, to borrow Kuhn's useful, but now fairly dog-eared term, the present stage may prove to be a valuable clearing of the decks for a new approach to social investigation, differing fundamentally in form and content from the approach developed during the positivist stages. I will suggest the possible lines for a new approach in a concluding chapter, but the extent of the opposition to any new programme can only be gauged by a fairly detailed scrutiny of the expanding universe of behavioural science in related fields. This scrutiny occupies the chapters which follow.

Notes to Chapter IV

1. 'Stochastic', is, of course, a comparative newcomer to the lexicon. The term appears only in the most up-to-date dictionaries of the social sciences, and has no separate entry in the *International Encyclopaedia of the Social Sciences* (New York, 1968, 17 vols.). The *Oxford English Dictionary* defines stochastic as 'pertaining to conjecture'; *Webster's Third New International* (1961 ed.) is ambivalent: 'skilful in aiming, proceeding by guesswork'. Cf., D. J. Bartholomew, *Stochastic Models for Social Processes* (London, 1973) for a less tentative viewpoint. The Greek root of the word makes 'guesswork' the correct meaning.

2. Maurice Halbwach made this point more than half a century ago in his critique of Quetelet's statistical figment, 'the common man'. See Halbwach's *Théorie de l'homme moyen: essai sur Quetelet et la Statistique Morale* (Alcan, 1913).

3. Samuel Stouffer *et al.*, *The American Soldier* (Studies in Social Psychology in World War II) (2 vols., Princeton, 1949), II, 77 ff.

4. Stouffer *et al., op. cit.* (II), pp. 77, 107 ff.

5. Paul Lazarsfeld and Allen Barton, 'Qualitative Measurement in the Social Sciences: Classification, Typologies and Indices'; in Daniel Lerner and Harold Lasswell, *The Policy Sciences* (Stanford, 1965), pp. 160 ff.

6. T. W. Adorno *et al.*, *The Authoritarian Personality* (1st ed. 1950). References given here are from the W. W. Norton ed. (New York, 1969).

7. Chap. 1, *op. cit.*, is a detailed methodological Introduction to the study.

8. Adorno, *op. cit.*, pp. 58 ff.

9. *Ibid.*, pp. 110–11.

10. *Ibid.*, p. 103.

11. *Ibid.*, p. 229.

12. Clearly, it can be shown that after the collapse of Weimar, the worried middle classes of Germany accepted Nazism as the only available option to rescue them from total collapse. But the seed-bed of Nazism was in the beer halls and the street corners, among the unemployed – not in the more comfortable suburbs, as Adorno and associates postulate by implication.

13. *Ibid.*, p. 23.

14. *Ibid.*, p. 23. The terminal statement on 'additional' relationships is no more than the familiar escape hatch to

convey scholarly caution, or possibly to counter too meticulous a scrutiny of the research design and findings.

15. Cf. *Ibid.*, pp. 500–3, 901–4, *et passim*.

16. Dahrendorf's paper appeared first in the *American Journal of Sociology*, Vol. LXIV, No. 2 (1958) soon after Merton's *Social Theory and Social Structure* (1957), and is reprinted in Dahrendorf, *Essays in the Theory of Society* (London, 1968), pp. 107–28.

17. The literature on both sides of the Atlantic is now considerable and only a small portion can be cited. Among the more thought provoking, cf., W. G. Runciman's essays in *Sociology in its Place* (1970); Alvin Gouldner's *The Coming Crisis of Western Sociology* (1971), and his recent essays in *For Sociology* (1973); John Rex, *Discovering Sociology* (1973) and his recent *Sociology and the Demystification of the Modern World* (London, 1974). The continuing discussions in essays by Peter Winch, Ernest Gellner, Alasdair MacIntyre, Alan Ryan and the late Imre Lakatos are perhaps too familiar to need recounting. Some of the best papers are collected in the series edited by Runciman *et al.*, *Philosophy, Politics and Society* (Oxford, 1956 to date), and in Alan Ryan (ed.), *The Philosophy of Social Explanation* (Oxford, 1973). Kuhn's concept of the paradigm is set out in his *The Structure of Scientific Revolutions* (1st ed., 1962, 2nd ed., enlarged, Chicago, 1970) and there are useful critical discussions in several of the papers in Imre Lakatos and Alan Musgrave (eds.), *Criticism and the Growth of Knowledge* (Cambridge, 1970) including Kuhn's 'Reflections on my Critics', *ibid.*, pp. 231–78.

V

Game Theorists

Since its first publication in 1944, *The Theory of Games and Economic Behaviour* by J. von Neumann and Oskar Morgenstern has greatly influenced mathematical approaches to economics by providing new tools and theorems for the analysis of dynamic equilibrium patterns, in place of the old static equilibrium of classical economics. Game theory has also had an immense influence in cognate fields of decision-making, including strategic studies, conflict theory and systems analysis. As the co-authors stress in their opening technical note, the techniques employed in the theory of games are 'thoroughly mathematical', and stem directly from von Neumann's earlier papers in mathematical journals from 1928 onwards, in which the basis of the theory was first explored.[1] The 1944 text is an elegant masterpiece of abstract theory on mathematical principles. But it has very little to do with economic *behaviour*, despite the titular claim.

My criticisms of the theoretical framework of *The Theory of Games* are not from the point of view of internal consistency, but rather from the fundamental premises used for the construction of the theory. The theory requires, as a prime postulate, a definition of rationality on the part of the 'players' in any game or series of games. Now rationality is, both in logic and experience, quite distinct from the concept of utility as this has been defined in economic analysis.[2] But the distinction is blurred by von Neumann in order to secure a guiding definition for rationality within the theory of games. Von Neumann and Morgenstern acknowledge the problem in an opening chapter to their work, but their 'Qualitative discussion of the Problem of Rational Behaviour'[3] is extremely brief, and cannot be said to explore a problem on which whole treatises could, and already have been written.

They begin their brief treatment with the statement 'The subject matter of economic theory is the very complicated mechanism of prices and production, and of the gaining and spending of incomes' (p. 8). Most economists today would find this description limiting, and certainly incomplete. It is not so circumscribed as Francis Edgeworth's classic definition of the Economical Calculus, 'The first principle of Economics is that every agent is actuated only by self interest',[4] but the von Neumann definition is nevertheless circumscribed; a necessary device in order to identify rationality with no more than the maximisation of utilities.

Objections to the measurement of utilities, the authors argue (p. 16) are reminiscent of early objections to measurement in the theory of heat, since 'that too was based on the intuitively clear concept of one body feeling warmer than another, yet there was no immediate way to express significantly by how much, by how many times or in what sense'. Except, one might add, the device of placing mercury in a tube marked with a calibrated scale to register differences of heat. Even so, the analogy fails, since a thermometer measures body temperature and *not* how hot or cold a person may be *feeling* at a particular moment. Modern science has not so far invented a thermometer which registers one's utilities by placing a calibrated tube under the patient's tongue, so that they may be read off by trained economists. But if such a device should be invented, the utilities would be those of an abstracted 'economic man', whose preferences are merely the median points in a spectrum of possible utilities.

The opening chapter of *The Theory of Games* is thus an exercise in abstract analytics. From the assertion that 'there exists, at present, no satisfactory treatment of the question of rational behaviour' (p. 9), the authors proceed rapidly to provide an all-embracing theory of their own, which argues that rationality can be measured; and that the rational individual seeks to maximise his gains and minimise his losses. This crude bifurcation, which entails, for reasons of convenience and symmetry, that a gain can only be a gain, and a loss can only be a loss, and that one person's gain is another person's loss (and *vice versa*), is the curtain raiser for the elaborate exercises in mathematical reasoning which occupy the remaining 600 pages of *The Theory of Games*, and which includes the minimax principle as a vital part of the argument.

The minimax principle has spawned an immense literature not merely in economics, but in other fields such as conflict theory, international relations, group theory, and systems analysis.[5] Game theory itself has moved to new levels of sophistication since the *opus classicum* appeared in 1944, and it is fair to add that no competent theoretician would now investigate rationality in the crude, dichotomous terms referred to above. Nevertheless, game theory does promote a particular intellectual approach to problems, not so much in their solution, but in their formulation, and since solutions are always to some extent hostage to the questions asked, the effects can be fundamental. More particularly, game theoretical solutions are the prisoners of the matrix or matrices selected for elucidating supposed areas of choice operating within given constraints.

A familiar example will help. The best known two-person, non-zero-sum game in the literature is *Prisoner's Dilemma*. The precise terms of the game vary slightly in different texts on either side of the Atlantic, but the elements of the game are the same. I will set out the game in what seems to me the clearest form, and will go on to argue that the 'school' solution accepted in all extant texts is in fact not proven.[6] That the school solution should be accepted by leading scholars whose critical acumen is beyond question may owe something to the hypnotic effect of number.[7]

In *Prisoner's Dilemma* two persons, A and B, are held to be
guilty of a serious crime, but the available evidence is not
sufficient to convict them in open court. Held in custody, they
are told by the crown prosecutor (in the American version,
the district attorney) that they will be asked separately, and
incommunicado, to confess. If both confess, both will receive
a reduced sentence for confessing, say eight years. If neither
confesses, a minor charge will be preferred and they are each
liable to get two years. If one confesses and the other does
not, the confessor will receive an even lighter sentence for
assisting the law – say one year – whilst the non-confessor will
get ten years. What should each prisoner do – bearing in
mind that it is impossible to communicate with each other?

The accepted textbook solution is that it is in the interests
of each prisoner to confess. Both therefore get a sentence of
eight years. Their respective strategies can be set out in a
simple matrix thus:

Prisoner B

		Not confess	*Confess*
Prisoner A	*Not confess*	2, 2.	10, 1.
	Confess	1, 10.	8, 8.

The relative severities of sentence facing each prisoner are
shown. The textbook solution is that self-seeking will prompt
A and B to confess, in order to ensure a sentence of eight years
as the maximum possible – whatever the other prisoner does
– rather than not confess, with the possibility (if the other
confesses) of ten years. Thus the argument proceeds on the
basis of self-interest as 'rationality'. I will suggest that even
accepting such a basis, both prisoners will be moved *not* to
confess, and that the textbook solution – not to mention the
extensive literature built on that 'solution' – is false.

A common characteristic of any game in game theory is
that closed systems must be assumed, and that the 'rules of

the game' (e.g. no communication, bargains or deals) are prescribed. Let us grant these conditions for *Prisoner's Dilemma*. Thus it is not permissible to allow one or both prisoners to conjecture whether, after confessing, the district attorney/crown prosecution will renege on the initial assurance and award a heavy punishment to fit the confessed crime. Such a possibility lies outside the 'rules' of the game. Nevertheless, this game, like other games in game theory, has built into it certain assumptions and rules of inference which must be allowed so that it qualifies as a game, and not purely and simply an exercise in comparative numerical magnitudes. In *Prisoner's Dilemma* the principal built-in assumption is that each player will act selfishly, so as to maximise his gains. But if each player does so act then clearly his individual preference (and maximum utility) is non-confession, so as to secure the light sentence of two years, rather than the eight he earns for confessing. However, the 'rules' insists, egoism *also* entails that each player distrusts the other, so that confession is the safest course in order to avoid the possibility of a ten year sentence, should the other confess.

But to think, or conjecture about the other person's actions and motives is an intellectual step which leads logically to the recognition of a mutuality of interest. There is a common predicament. Self-regard prompts the recognition of this on the part of both prisoners, to an equal degree. But if Prisoner A and Prisoner B devote so much as a moment to thinking of the other's likely course of action, then the logic of such a consideration is that both appreciate equally that the rational course of action is for both separately (but in the outcome jointly), to maximise their *possible* gains by not confessing.

Hence, three separate paths of reasoning lead directly to the decision of both prisoners not to confess.

(*1*) *Blind* egoism, in which no thought whatever is given to the other prisoner's possible choice. Under these terms, non-confession is the choice, since it is aiming at a *possible* very light sentence of two years, as opposed to eight years or ten years.

(*2*) *Reasoned* egoism, in which each prisoner seeks to minimise the likelihood of a heavy sentence by acting in the way he expects the other prisoner to act (that is, from self-interest) in the identical situation in which he finds himself. Since their situation is identical, and since the rules of the game pose identical processes of reasoning, it is more rational for both to aim at a sentence of two years, rather than a sentence of eight years. Therefore neither confesses.

(*3*) *Reasoned altruism*, in which each prisoner again acts out of self-interest, but each realises that if he acts purely out of self-interest this is self defeating, since he is opting for eight years instead of a possible two year sentence. By recognising that the other prisoner's dilemma is no greater, and no less than his own, it is rational to see that both recognise this equally (as the rules of the game allow), and that self-interest is coterminous with mutual interest. Again, then, neither prisoner confesses.

One may comment more generally on the type of reasoning deployed in the accepted textbook 'solution' to the game, in which both prisoners confess. It identifies rationality with the maximum mutual distrust, rather than with the minimum mutual self-interest. The cultural implications of rationality-as-distrust are interesting enough for further comment, but my concern here is with techniques of argument, rather than the philosophical and social implications behind them. Defenders of the accepted solution might argue that in some texts, *Prisoner's Dilemma* is defined as a 'non-co-operative' game – but if this means that no other element than non-co-operation is present, then it ceases to have any validity as a game, and becomes something else – that is, an attempt to arrange the maximum sentence for the other prisoner, rather than the minimum sentence for oneself. The two aims lead to different solutions. Inflicting the maximum possible sentence on the other prisoner inescapably involves confessing. Aiming at the likeliest minimum sentence for oneself entails not confessing, given the *ceteris paribus* rules of the game.

I conclude that the 'school' solution to *Prisoner's Dilemma* is false, and the very considerable literature erected on that solution is fallacious. Where applications of game theory based on the simple minimax criteria have resulted in policy decisions by governments, or those advising governments, one may be disturbed at what results or has resulted. Game theory sees society as composed of individuals and groups with mutually opposed sets of interests. Rationality is defined as exclusive self-interest. Society is thus a war of each against each, and of all against all.

There are signs that this disastrously limiting definition of rationality is giving way to concepts of 'collective rationality' rather than the abstracted individual 'rationality' of classical game theory.[8] But the proponents of 'n-person' game theory, as distinct from two person game theory, have not so far provided any acceptable definition or refinement of 'collective rationality.' Elements of co-operation, and the study of bargaining and other forms of collective action, are now admitted to the matrix. What is not conceded is that whilst the matrix may portray, artificially if elegantly, the supposed choices of abstracted 'rational' persons, these choices have no necessary connection with, or application to, the logic of choice in the real world.

Notes to Chapter V

1. For reasons of convenience and space I will refer only to von Neumann as the principal author in the following discussion without, I hope, derogating from Morgenstern's contribution.
2. Rationality is, needless to say, a complex topic in its own right, which has justly claimed a good deal of attention from philosophers, social anthropologists and many social scientists. Cf. Bryan Wilson's valuable collection of papers *Rationality* (Oxford, 1970) especially the papers by Steven Lukes, Martin Hollis and Peter Winch. See also Alasdair MacIntyre, *Against the Self-Images of the Age* (London, 1971), pp. 244–59; and Alfred Schutz, 'The Problem of Rationality in the Social World', in Dorothy Emmet and Alasdair MacIntyre (eds.), *Sociological Theory and Philosophical Analysis* (London, 1970).

3. *Theory of Games*, pp. 8–9.
4. Edgeworth's remark appeared in his monograph *Mathematical Psychics* (London, 1881). Excerpts are reprinted in William J. Baumol and Stephen M. Goldfeld, *Precursors in Mathematical Economics* (London School of Economics, *Reprints of Scarce Works on Political Economy*, No. 19, London, 1968), pp. 192–200.
5. The American historian and strategic theorist Bernard Brodie has pointed out that a high proportion of those who have made their mark on strategic theory and conflict theory in the United States have been trained as economists, and the influence of Game Theory is clear in their writings. See Brodie, 'The Scientific Strategists' in R. Gilpin and C. Wright (eds.), *Scientists and National Policy Making* (New York, 1964), p. 247.
6. The game is attributed to A. W. Tucker and can be found in most manuals on game theory. See A. Rapoport and A. M. Chammah, *Prisoner's Dilemma* (Ann Arbor, 1965); A. Rapoport, *Fights, Games and Debates* (Ann Arbor, 1960) *passim*, R. Duncan Luce and H. Raiffa, *Games and Decisions* (New York, 1957), pp. 95 ff., Articles on 'Prisoner's Dilemma' are legion: a review of the literature on this game is given by P. S. Gallo and C. McClintock in *Journal of Conflict Resolution*, 9 (1965), pp. 68–78.
7. Examples of this acceptance occur in a valuable paper by W. G. Runciman and A. K. Sen, *'Games, Justice and the General Will'* which first appeared in *Mind*, ns., LXXIV (1965), and is reprinted in W. G. Runciman, *Sociology in its Place, and Other Essays* (Cambridge, 1970), pp. 224–32. See also John Rawls, *A Theory of Justice* (1972), p. 269, fn., and for a more general acceptance of game theory postulates, R. B. Braithwaite, *Theory of Games as a Tool for the Moral Philosopher* (Cambridge, 1955).
8. Rapoport has moved on to 'n-person' game theory, taking note of T. C. Schelling's contribution in his *Strategy of Conflict* (1962). Cf. Anatol Rapoport, *Game Theory as a Theory of Conflict Resolution* (Boston & Dordrecht, 1974).

VI
Economic Imperialists

One of the most striking developments in economics in recent years has been the revival of interest in welfare economics. The reasons are many, but among them one can note the need to plot the welfare function, especially in the mixed economy, where government decisions affect social choice; the interrelated problems of full employment and inflation; and the political and ethical problems these bring with them. The inflationary spiral, in which the dominant problem for governments is how to get the correct mix of demand management, fiscal measures, savings and investment whilst maintaining full employment, has complicated the debate and introduced lively controversy, including a reassessment of Keynes.[1]

A good deal of the discussion has focused on the unsatisfactory nature of Paretian criteria of optimality. The Pareto criterion may be expressed in different ways, with both strong and weak affirmations of the cardinal principle.[2] Put very simply, however, it asserts that if a particular change in the economy leaves at least one individual better off, and no individual worse off, social welfare may be said to have increased. Application of the principle constantly comes up against problems of how individual preferences are to be measured, possible substitution effects and the effect of government measures on preference scales. Theoretical models are constructed, and whilst optimality is not too complicated a matter to represent in the simple model where the basic elements are the perfectly competitive system, private goods, and no externalities, problems start up on all sides when these conditions are breached, as they must be in any application of the model.

In the real world, preferences must be expressed by individuals and groups, and decisions must be taken by governments in conditions of uncertainty. Very often the most that can be achieved is second best – a notion which now claims a significant portion of the literature.[3] Redefining optimality is thus a controversial activity and two broad schools can be identified, the theoretical and the empirical. The division is by no means clearcut but nevertheless a distinction can be made between the formal, axiomatic approach of, say, A. K. Sen (using set theory), or of Kenneth Arrow and J. de V. Graaff on the one hand, and the recent discussion by Rowley and Peacock on the other.[4]

What strikes an observer in the exchanges that have gone on, roughly speaking, since I. M. D. Little's *A Critique of Welfare Economics* (1950), is that for one group welfare economics is a theoretical discourse, free from the contagion of value judgements. For the other group, welfare theory that does not admit its initial value premises, and which makes no contact with the real world of social choices, is a form of elegant dilettantism. In constructing their models the pure theorists simplify political constitutions into artificial abstractions such as 'ideal' dictatorships, or into democracies where voters are presented with clear sets of either/or alternatives, rather than the muddy sets of compromises which are the norm of every democratic society, for endogenous and exogenous reasons.

One part of the literature is thus increasingly abstract, and econometric in form and content, even when the topic under discussion is essentially normative. An example occurs in A. K. Sen's discussion of Equity and Justice.[5] There is an initial attempt to examine Kant's categorical imperatives, by reference to Sidgwick's utilitarianism. Sen then briefly takes up Rawls' concept of justice as fairness, not in order to develop a philosophical argument, but rather to transpose Rawls' argument into a set of orderings and quasi-orderings. Sen escapes into this mathematical treatment by asserting:

> For the use of the Rawls criterion of justice, measurability of individual welfare is not really necessary, not even in the ordinal sense. The criterion can be presented in terms of orderings, and discussions on it can take place perfectly well without bringing in welfare measures at all.[6]

Sen thus devotes a whole chapter (Chapter 9) to taking the welfare criterion out of Rawls' argument and formalising it in terms of set theory. What he distinctly fails to do is to join the argument put forward by Rawls in the way that, for instance, Barry does in his closely argued critique.[7]

Professor Rawls' theory of justice has now been worked over by so many economists, particularly those wishing to modify, update, or escape from the Paretian criteria of optimality, that Rawls must wonder whether his work is any longer his own, even though the attention must be flattering.[8]

Sen's rendering of Rawls' argument into a set of mathematical orderings will be defended, no doubt, as a legitimate attempt to simplify the assumptions; present them with greater clarity and rigour than ordinary discourse allows. As such, it takes its place within a developing tendency of economists – but particularly of mathematical economists – to go outside the traditional bounds of their discipline in ambitious attempts to clarify, and if possible to bring greater rigour to discussions or debates in other disciplines.

This brings us to the general charge of 'Economic Imperialism', a topic on which some economists are sufficiently sensitive to recognise the term and to discuss the charge. In defence of the imperialist tendency, Gordon Tullock in an essay entitled 'Economic Imperialism' chides political scientists for failing to recognise the importance of Anthony Downs' work *An Economic Theory of Democracy*.[9] Tullock suggests (*loc. cit.*) that most political scientists will find the book hard going, and that they would 'probably find it necessary to devote six months to a year to acquiring the necessary intellectual capital in the form of a good background in economics'.

This admonishment, which provides interesting clues to a *de haut en bas*, if not an imperialist frame of mind (Professor Tullock's tone is shrill throughout his essay) comes a little late to at least one of Professor Tullock's readers. I read the book without difficulty some years ago, and dismissed it, I regret to say, as a singularly unhelpful exploration of a field where Downs' competence is, to say the least, debatable.

However, Downs' book does provide a useful example of what occurs when model builders whose primary training is in economics seek to construct models in other disciplines where the simplifying assumptions of economic model building are hazardous in the extreme. Apart from the simplifications Downs must make for the construction of his model (to be discussed further below), his prime postulate is, as it must be, rationality on the part of governments and voters. He therefore needs a definition, or definitions, of rationality before he sets out to construct his model. He begins with an ingenious argument (p. 4) that since economic theorists 'have nearly always looked at decisions as though they were made by rational minds' and again, that 'economic theory has been erected upon the supposition that conscious rationality prevails', it therefore follows *ipso facto* that an economic theory of democracy – Downs' purpose – is plausible. The form of the argument speaks for itself. It also begs so many prior questions, and contains so many breath-taking assumptions, that it seems best to allow Downs to proceed to the next stage of his model construction without further comment.

The economist's working definition of rationality as least input of scarce resources per unit of valued output is taken up, and Downs stresses that for his model, as for economic models, such extraneous considerations as conflicting ends, alternative satisfactions and/or preferences, or substitution effects, cannot be admitted into the basic model. Thus, as Downs readily concedes, his political man 'remains an abstraction from the real fullness of the human personality' (p. 7). Political man, in the Downs model, thus possesses a built-in 'psychic economy' (the term is Downs') whose 'rational behaviour' makes him approach every decision or choice 'with one eye on the gains to be had, the other eye on costs, a delicate ability to balance them, and a strong desire to follow wherever rationality leads him'.

So far, so simplified. As for governments, there are necessary simplifications here also. Taking the orthodox democratic model, with periodic elections laid down by the constitution, and with majority rule, every government seeks to maximise political support. Election or re-election as governing party (or leading partner in a coalition) is the chief goal. These initial assumptions (p. 11) are uncontroversial. Having made them, Downs promptly introduces the crucial simplifications required for his model (p. 12).

> The governing party thus has unlimited freedom of action, within the bounds of the constitution . . . Economically, there are no limits to its power. It can nationalize everything, or hand everything over to private parties, or strike any balance between these extremes. It can impose any taxes and carry out any spending it desires. The only restraint upon it is that of maintaining political freedom; therefore it must not vitiate its opponents by economic policies aimed specifically at injuring them. Also it must economically uphold the voting rights of its citizens.

At this point, the student of politics can only conjecture at the *Alice in Wonderland* aspects of Professor Downs' theoretical democracy. Begging the question of how governments *economically* uphold voting rights, we are to assume that the government can nationalise everything, including all private property (presumably, even sell the individuals' property to foreign dealers), introduce a dozen new taxes, spend what it likes on any programme it chooses, with the proviso only that this package of government actions maintains political freedom for its citizens and does not injure the chances of other parties.

By political freedom, Professor Downs appears to mean no more than the freedom to vote, and the inability of the government to tamper with the constitution – for instance on the holding of elections. But if political freedom is defined in such narrow terms, and if these simplifications are coupled with the simplifications already introduced, not least the abstracted 'rational' voter (in Downs' unusual definition) the utility of the model becomes even more conjectural.

The model proceeds to a discussion of propositions and hypotheses. These strike me as either trivial or impossible to prove or disprove within the terms of the model.

For example:

Proposition: The parties in a coalition government are under simultaneous pressures to converge and diverge ideologically (p. 143).

Proposition: A certain amount of political irrationality is inevitable in any society (p. 143).

Proposition: In an uncertain world, rational decision makers acquire only a limited amount of information before making choices (p. 207).

Downs may argue that none of these propositions is self-evident, and that they need to be tested. One can only reply that these propositions are either trivial, or self-evident within the context and meaning of such terms as 'coalition', 'society', 'uncertain world'. If this is denied, then no basis for argument or discussion can exist, since there is fundamental disagreement on terminology here, as there must also be on Downs' narrowly construed definition of rationality. At such a point, the only course is to move to the final propositions contained in the book (pp. 296–300) so that we may assess the theoretical scheme put forward. The propositions asserted again seem to me to have certain dominant characteristics: they are self-evident by definition or trivial, or so hypothetical and abstracted, that the reverse proposition is equally plausible.

Proposition: In a two-party system, party policies are (a) more vague (b) more similar to those of other parties [*sic*] and (c) less directly linked to an ideology than in a multiparty system (p. 297).

Proposition: Under certain circumstances, a rational man votes for a party other than the one he would most prefer to see in office (p. 298).

Proposition: Political parties tend to carry out as many of their promises as they can whenever they are elected (p. 300).

I have dwelt on Downs' *An Economic Theory of Democracy* not from any particular desire to question an honest attempt to introduce model-building into political studies, but to raise more general and fundamental issues concerning the purview of economics as a discipline. Economic theorists have fashioned certain tools of inquiry which may or may not (the debate must be conducted by economists themselves) fit well with their discipline. But it becomes extremely hazardous when such concepts as 'rationality' (narrowly defined as maximising possible gains for minimum input per unit) are exported to other types of behaviour – especially those in which ethical and political considerations *must* be present *by specification of the problem to be discussed*. It is difficult to analyse a candidate's qualifications for the priesthood if it is first specified that since religious convictions introduce uncertainties and imponderables into the analysis, these must be ruled out *ab initio* and deemed to be irrelevant for establishing criteria for a suitable 'model', with predictive capacity. This is not to say that a candidate totally lacking in religious convictions may not increase church attendance at his benefice; more than, say, another candidate whose *chief* characteristic is religious conviction, but this at the cost of qualities more suited to Trade Union organisation, or an election day rally. It is merely to say that minimax criteria are not always the most suitable guides for arriving at testable propositions, and beyond these to policy decisions.

Clearly, most economists are very conscious of the need for caution when building models on the basis of simplified assumptions – both within their own discipline and, by implication, outside it. There is abundant evidence that most economists find crude minimax criteria entirely insufficient. Others, however, are neither apologetic nor repentant, since they regard economic theory, and even economic analysis, as having special characteristics denied to other forms of inquiry. Professor Buchanan makes his own position clear in an essay appropriately titled 'Toward Analysis of Closed Behavioural Systems'.[10]

> The appropriate response of the economist to such criticism should be (but perhaps too rarely has been) that he is wholly unconcerned, as a professional scientist, about the ethically relevant characteristics of the behavior that he examines. To the extent that men behave as his model predicts, the economist can explain uniformities in social order. To the extent that men behave differently, his predictions are falsified. It is as simple as that.[11]

This places the activity of model-building on a 'heads we win, tails you lose' basis if one wants to join the argument on the status and validity of model-building (present *and* future). However, this opens up a vast discussion and most established economists have long since taken up their positions in an ancient debate. It is not my purpose to enter an arena from which most of the contestants have withdrawn, all more or less satisfied that they have jousted successfully and carried off some if not all of the prizes. But it does strike an outsider, after a fresh, if incomplete immersion in the literature, that economics seems more than ever likely to separate into two distinctive sub-disciplines, the one formal, axiomatic, deductive, and belonging peculiarly to the world of pure mathematics; the other stressing that economics is an applied social science, or it is nothing. The second group cannot be dismissed as innumerate, since their work elegantly testifies the opposite, but they clearly find it more congenial to locate their work in an intellectual tradition cognate to other disciplines, especially philosophy and politics, rather than across the divide between pure science and the humanistic disciplines. And it is surely more in keeping with the essential nature and purpose of scholarly inquiry – undogmatic, making due allowance for one's subjective prejudices, taking into account alternative sets of convictions as these are seen, or held by other people – and to recognise these elements, so that due allowance can be made for them, rather than to disregard them as either irrelevant, or likely to impair the rigour of the analysis by introducing extraneous or recalcitrant elements.

Some economists are less confident than others that they can, or even should, avoid the ethical dimensions of their work. Gunnar Myrdal has pointed out that in his work on development problems in South Asia, and in his classic work on the American Negro, hidden biases in the existing literature were the chief problem in meeting his terms of reference. For his work on South Asia, he found that 'all principal concepts, theories, and models have been biased, both in colonial times and after the Second World War . . .'[12] These biases were caused principally by the influences of diplomacy, but also by 'wishful thinking' in the context of the Cold War. But equally seriously, Myrdal argues, were the biases introduced by 'the uncritical application of scientific approaches worked out for economic analysis in the Western developed countries'.[13] The results were often faulty policy conclusions based on false perceptions of reality.

Economists, then, are the prisoners of social, intellectual, and political conditioning. To the extent that they deny this, or fail to allow for it in their researches, to that extent the distortions in their work may be greater, not less. Thus the first step in the specification of a problem to be investigated is to set out the value premises the researcher brings to the inquiry. It is then, and only then, that the researcher can begin to show that in the methods he adopts, his approach may be more objective than other approaches, which is not to say that he will, in the end, secure increased objectivity, since there is a concealed equation, awaiting demonstration, between his initial value premises, his adopted method, and his conclusions.

These considerations apply to the macro level of theory, but also to the levels of micro-analysis. Here, the discussion can usefully turn on the immense variety of analytical work in cost-benefit analysis now available in a burgeoning literature. Projects cover all aspects of economic investigation, from the location of airports to urban renewal projects, from public health and allocation of resources in public sector studies to projects in the private sector.

One can as easily point to excellent work in, for instance, health economics, as to unfortunate lapses such as the Roskill Commission on the Third London Airport.[14] Advocates of cost-benefit analysis argue that its prime virtue is to clarify choices, both public and private. They would claim no special expertise in the *evaluation* of choices to be made – a new airport versus an urban renewal programme or a new hospital building programme, for instance – but they would necessarily insist that governments or individuals can make better – because more informed – choices once the evidence is presented to them.

However cost-benefit analysis, like welfare economics and the economics of growth, plunges quickly into politics immediately choices have to be made, and different sets of questions can produce different answers. Who will benefit most, who least from the choice between alternative proposals? What are the social and psychological costs, as distinct from the *economic* costs to individuals or groups? Questions start up on all sides. What weighting should be given to a well-organised, articulate, middle-class pressure group, as against the inarticulate, or inchoate reactions of less educated sections of the population, perhaps greater in number, but much less vocal in their opposition to a particular proposal?

Cost-benefit specialists are more aware of these problems now than they were some years ago. However, they cannot forgo a basic technique of the method, which is to assign numerical values to costs and benefits in order to discover finally – however sophisticated the analysis – whether costs exceed benefits, or vice versa. Here, the Pareto criterion of optimality (support a project if some people gain, and nobody loses) appeals to some. The Kaldor-Hicks criterion (support a project if the gainers can compensate the losers, even if they do not) appeals to others. A whole treatise could be written on the social and political implications of the second part of the Kaldor-Hicks criterion, *'even if they do not'*, but putting this aside, cost-benefit analysts are familiar with the technical problems encountered at every stage of their estimations, from market imperfections and externalities, the shadow pricing of market items, fluctuations in exchange rates and (in recent years) varying rates of inflation, to a host of endogenous factors affecting opportunity costs, social preferences, individual preferences, and redistribution effects, all of them heavy with political overtones. As Prest and Turvey state in the classic survey article, we encounter here an 'algebraic jungle of constructing decision algorithms'.[15]

To the claim, then, that decisions based on cost-benefit analysis are better than those which are not, since the former are based on more reliable information, or at least on a greater amount and/or variety of information objectively analysed, we must put the prior question, 'What type of information?' On balance the answer must be, that information which is most easily quantified, even where these are responses from the public, or from sections of the public, in questionnaires. In most cases, however, the quantified data relate to money values and costs and there is a necessary assumption, in the absence of contradictory evidence, that to persons *in the same income bracket*, a person A places the same value on £1 as a person B. It is also a necessary assumption that persons with the same socio-economic characteristics place an equal value on, say, leisure time, or absence of pollution, or rapid communications by land, sea or air. Aggregation thus requires assumptions of uniformity so that, as in the Roskill Commission on the third London airport, the cost of businessmen's time in getting to and from the airport is averaged out, and assumptions made on comparative costs of *time* for other travellers. As Mishan has pointed out, the central assumptions of Roskill were highly questionable, and the fact that supersonic travel was not envisaged, or taken into account (so that today analysis would be fundamentally affected by environmental aspects of the location, as well as much reduced travel time in the air) made Roskill a singularly unhelpful exercise. Clearly, one swallow does not make a summer, and one bad example cannot damage successful estimations elsewhere. However, Mishan makes the point that in such economic calculations, considerations of social equity are very largely ignored. He notes that if the business tycoons and holiday-makers are shown to benefit to such an extent that they *could* more than compensate the victims of aircraft spillover (on the Kaldor-Hicks criterion), then the cost-benefit criterion is met. But compensation is *not* paid: the former continue to enjoy sporadic profit or pleasure, whilst the latter continuously and permanently suffer the disamenities.

One can go further, and make a more fundamental objection – that the cost-benefit criterion is itself the culprit if methodological practice habituates economists to believing that preferences can be measured which are, in principle, not susceptible to measurement, either individually or collectively in the mix of public and private amenities and disamenities in the mixed economy. An individual has distinctive sets of utilities according to what preoccupies him at a particular moment. We are all familiar with the impatient motorist who curses pedestrians for crossing busy streets or holding up the flow of traffic. We are also familiar with the pedestrian who curses the motor-car for causing congestion, ruining the environment, and causing danger to life and limb. Needless to say, most of us are both types of person at different times of the day or week, whilst others may be one *or* the other, and others again dislike both the motor car, and crowded shopping centres, and the general devil-take-the-hindmost drift of modern society.

Who or what is responsible for that general drift? It is difficult to argue that those *least* responsible are those who have provided governments, local government, and decision makers with cost-benefit analyses showing, for instance, that high rise housing and prefabricated building techniques cut costs; that urban motorways such as those now disfiguring many city centres (which no longer have city centres) speed traffic circulation, and therefore improve modern living standards; or that schools built for, say, 2,000 pupils are more cost effective than schools for 200 pupils.

Si monumentum requiris, circumspice. The new concern, among economists as among others, for introducing other criteria than over-simplified ones of maximum benefits for minimum costs, is very much overdue. If there is a new concern for 'the quality of life' this implies that the past concern was with quantity as the benchmark in the production of goods and services. If 'Growth-mania' is now on the way out, experts in economic growth have made past errors whose origin lies within the discipline and its methods, and not in the personal characteristics of economists, who are ordinary citizens like the rest of the population, whatever claims are made for the importance of the discipline within the context of government, or local or institutional bureaucracies.

It will be argued that cost-benefit analysis, like other forms of economic analysis, attempts to do no more than clarify the options: it is for governments, or other decision-makers to take the decision on which of the options to take up. But my argument here is that by its methods, its primary reliance on minimax criteria, and even, let it be admitted frankly, by virtue of claims to superior numeracy explicit or implicit (a vital persuasion in government departments or local town halls, where innumeracy is not uncommon) economic analysis forecloses some options ('costs outweigh benefits') and impels decision makers to favour others ('benefits outweigh costs'), wherever the financial constraints are among the chief factors present.

To point out the institutional effects, at every level, of cost-benefit analysis is not to deny its importance or efficacy. Economists are right to conclude that much of the animus directed against 'the dismal science' in Carlyle's phrase, or against 'sophisters, economists and calculators' in Burke's equally prejudiced comment, stem from ignorance, malice, or a mixture of the two.

The doubts and caveats I have expressed here do not, I would hope, spring from either of those motives, but rather from a sense that economic analysis, because of its technical content, is likely to contribute a lion's share to the decision making processes affecting our daily lives in what is, undeniably, a very technical and technological era. What is necessary, perhaps, is a recognition on the part of economists, but more particularly of econometricians, that there are certain sorts of questions for which they have a special, indeed a unique competency; there are other sorts of questions and problems to which their talents are less suited, and there are others again where they are floundering in the philosophical abyss that lies between fact and value, between an 'is' and an 'ought'. In this regard, the flight to mathematical notation reveals, rather than conceals the basic incapacity.

It is understandable that different economists should show different intellectual preference scales in their approach to complex problems, and some will naturally prefer the sanctuaries (more apparent than real) of set theory, matrix algebra, or topology. Others are clearly more willing to risk their intellectual capital in the uncertain ventures of value judgements. The internal debate is best settled within the specialism itself, but in the meantime, if economics is indeed an applied science, it must be judged by the effects of its application, not by the elegance of its theorems.

Notes to Chapter VI

1. I am necessarily condensing here an extensive discussion within the profession as the old Pigovian approach to welfare was overtaken by Keynsianism, followed in turn by a spirited debate in the early 1950s between Kenneth Arrow, I. M. D. Little and others on the welfare function and theories of social choice, with earlier contributions by Scitovsky on welfare propositions in economics, and William Baumol's *Welfare Economics and the Theory of the State* (1952).

2. Cf. D. M. Winch, *Analytical Welfare Economics* (London, 1971, 1973), Chap. 4; E. S. Phelps (ed.), *Economic Justice* (London, 1973), p. 12. The definition I adopt here is the succinct one given in Charles K. Rowley and Alan T. Peacock, *Welfare Economics: A Liberal Restatement* (London, 1975), pp. 7–8, though needless to say the authors would be the first to stress that caveats must be entered once the criterion is under discussion.

3. R. G. Lipsey and K. Lancaster, 'The General Theory of Second Best', *Review of Economic Studies*, Vol. 24 (1956–7), pp. 11–32. For further discussion see E. J. Mishan (ed.), *Welfare Economics* (New York, 1969), pp. 72 ff., and Winch, *op. cit., passim*.

4. Charles K. Rowley and Alan T. Peacock, *op. cit.*

5. Amartya K. Sen, *Collective Choice and Social Welfare* (London, 1970), Chap. 9.*

6. *Ibid.*, p. 137, fn. 9.

7. Brian Barry, *The Liberal Theory of Justice: A Critical Examination of the Principal Doctrines in 'A Theory of Justice' by John Rawls* (Oxford, 1973).

8. I will cite here only the latest (to date) of many articles on Rawls, from the standpoint of a mathematical economist. Steven Strasnick, 'The Problem of Social Choice: Arrow to Rawls' (with acknowledgments to Arrow), *Philosophy and Public Affairs*, Vol. 5 (no. 3), 1976, pp. 241–73.

9. Tullock in James Buchanan and Robert Tollison (eds.), *Theory of Public Choice* (Ann Arbor, 1972), pp. 317–29; and Downs, *An Economic Theory of Democracy* (New York, 1957).

10. Buchanan and Tollison, *op. cit.*, pp. 11–23.

11. *Ibid.*, p. 17.

12. Gunnar Myrdal, *Objectivity in Social Research* (London, 1970), p. 45.

13. *Ibid.*, pp. 46 ff.

14. Cf. E. J. Mishan, *What Is Wrong With Roskill?* (1970). Reprinted
    in Richard Layard (ed.), *Cost-Benefit Analysis* (London, 1972,
    revised edn. 1974).
15. A. R. Prest and R. Turvey, 'The Main Questions' in Layard, *op.
    cit.*, p. 97.

VII
Psephologists

A good deal of discussion and disagreement has flowed between the 'behavioural' school of political science and what are variously termed the 'traditional', 'intuitionist' or 'normative' approaches to political studies.[1] The debate reached a watershed in the early 1960s, since when something in the nature of an undeclared truce has been maintained. Thoroughgoing behaviouralists have followed their own line, with increasing degrees of mathematical sophistication, bolstered by the readiness of learned journals to incorporate their contributions of work. At the same time there is a greater readiness to accept that earlier hopes for a value-free, truly 'scientific' study of political behaviour were over-optimistic, that politics both as *praxis* and as an intellectual discipline is peculiarly concerned with the interplay of normative judgements. In short, the self-styled 'behavioural revolution' has turned out not to be such, but rather an accretion or appendage to the study of politics, which different schools regard with different degrees of favour and disfavour. In the United States, where the new approaches were (and still are), most strongly entrenched, a revival of interest in political theory and normative discourse is occurring in some centres.[2]

In the face of these compromises, any discussion of the 'behavioural' approach to political studies has something of the flavour of silent battlefields where cohorts no longer exchange shot and shell. The academy − especially the American academy − is capacious enough to accommodate all sorts and conditions of political scientists, and since most social scientists sensibly prefer the quiet life to protracted ferment, the exchanges are now muted.

The second main development has been the tendency for those specialising in mathematical approaches to migrate, both conceptually and geographically, to areas most suited to their special skills. Voting behaviour, election studies and legislative behaviour (especially roll-call votes) is one area; cross-cultural comparison is another. In all cases, the wealth of available data allows behaviouralists to occupy themselves fully, with no shortage of materials for intellectual stimulation and fulfilment.

Students of politics who are not of the behavioural persuasion can be too dismissive of the mathematical analysis of political behaviour, using quantitative techniques. Here, as elsewhere, valuable explorations co-exist with ambitious trivia. The late V. O. Key's magisterial *Southern Politics in State and Nation* (1949), makes more demands on the ordinary reader than, say, Bagehot's *English Constitution* or Graham Wallas's *Human Nature in Politics*, but it is no less rich in insight, historical grasp and the capacity to further our understanding of political circumstance at the most fundamental level. But Key knew the limitations as well as the potentialities of statistical methods in the study of politics.[3] Elsewhere a greater degree of scepticism, or at the very least of caution in the use of, for example, public opinion surveys, election forecasts and the software of psephology can be noted.[4]

These are welcome and timely developments, though they are essentially refinements of method, rather than re-appraisals, and it is fair to add that their authors see no need for any re-appraisal. Rather the reverse, indeed, and it would be a foolhardy Canute who attempted to turn back the oceans of poll-findings and survey data which now support the researches of modern political science. It is possible, nevertheless, to draw back from what is now a vast investigative industry in order, once more, to discuss some of the fundamental postulates and pre-suppositions on which it is based. I will start with a consideration of public opinion.

So many books, tracts, pamphlets, and learned articles have resulted from the modern study of public opinion that apprentice political scientists can be forgiven (as the reading public can be forgiven) for overlooking the fact that public opinion does not exist. It is an artefact, constructed from the published findings of aggregated responses. It can be said to exist only in the metaphysical sense that the brotherhood of man exists. A pollster asked to identify public opinion on a particular issue can do one of two things. He can gesture towards the landscape and declare that it exists 'Out there' (which does not furnish proof of existence or identity), or he can display the tabulated findings resulting from a questionnaire, or house-to-house sample. But these findings are not 'public opinion': they are *private responses* (not opinions), *obtained* (not volunteered), from *separate individuals* (not from the corporate mass.)

It is no sort of answer to this to argue that modern polling techniques discover the 'state' of public opinion since careful comparisons of the responses to scientifically selected samples of different cohorts in the population allow us to confirm the 'state' of 'public opinion'. This argument is circular. Such comparisons simply compound the error of supposing that a readily formed 'public opinion' (as distinct from private opinions) exists. A 'public' opinion exists in no place, at no time, on any particular topic.

Because 'the public' is composed of individuals, then, it does not follow that there is a 'public' opinion. Whenever an 'opinion' is obtained from an individual on a particular point – or on one point at a time – then that expressed opinion is taken out of the context of a set of opinions, beliefs, points of view and perspectives on many related topics, some of which may heavily qualify the particular opinion on the particular topic under investigation. It is not sufficient to say that this difficulty is met by devices such as latent structure analysis (already referred to above, p. 6), as developed by Lazarsfeld

and colleagues.[5] This method makes the blanket supposition
that items under scrutiny are made up of two – and two only –
components, one specific to the item, the other linked to a
'latent' factor, as determined by the researcher. For analytical
purposes the two are assumed to be independent of each
other, yet this assumption of independence is a crucial one;
the pre-selection, or invention of what is 'latent' and what is
manifest take us once more into metaphysics, and thus to
contexts in which even the most careful estimation of so-
called 'error terms' is verbal adornment rather than statistical
refinement.

Apart from problems in the extrapolation of opinions
outside the context in which they are held by the individual, a
second main objection concerns the time element. Opinion
takers and survey researchers are conscious of the problem,
and have developed intricate techniques for the analysis of
trends. The time span may cover two or three years, tracing,
say, the formation of electoral opinion, or much longer time
spans, as in research projects tracing the effects of environment, social background, education and other effects on
groups of children, from infancy to adulthood.

Clearly, those occupied with the analysis of opinions are
aware that a one-off sampling of present 'opinion' is
unreliable as a guide to future opinion, but there is no clear
or satisfactory answer to what constitutes an acceptable time
span, or number of samplings, in order to analyse a definite
trend. By definition, a trend is a trend is a trend. The problem
is most acute in the area of political opinion. The most
obvious example is the public opinion poll of voting
intentions. The experiences of the polls in the United States
Presidential election of 1948, and of the British General
Elections of 1970 and 1974 have provided a good deal of
comment. In explaining – or explaining away – wrong
forecasts, pollsters took refuge in the assumption that late
surges of support came to Mr. Harry Truman in 1948, and to
Mr. Heath and the Conservative Party in 1970.[6]

In the 1970 British election result, this claim is backed up
by citing the one poll (ORC) which came very close to the

actual result. Since ORC re-interviewed a sub-sample (of only 300 voters, it is important to note) and found a late swing to the Conservatives, this was generalised to all other voters to account for a surprise result.[7] But this assumption is not necessarily supported by the facts, since alternative explanations are possible. ORC could have hit on the right result by a bias in its sampling techniques (see footnote 7, p. 74). If, on the other hand, ORC were to claim that its methods of sampling and questionnaire were not different *in kind* (one can quibble about the refinements of sampling techniques) from unsuccessful polls, such an explanation may be just as legitimate as the thesis of a very late swing. The thesis of a late swing can neither be proved nor disproved by the result of one re-interview of one sub-sample – since it rests on the assumption that previous polling results had specified degrees of accuracy, even though these cannot be established one way or the other. Thus, the assumption that one poll rescued the reputation of the other four polls in 1970 does not bear close scrutiny, though not surprisingly the polling organisations made ingenious attempts to rescue their reputations.

National Opinion Polls (NOP), Marplan and Gallup held post-mortems on their failure to get the result right by re-interviewing portions of the earlier sample. The technique was to select portions of the original sample and compare or contrast voting intention – whether declared, not declared or 'Don't Know', with the way votes were cast on polling day. Response rates for this 'follow up' were 55 per cent in the case of Marplan, 69 per cent for NOP. This raises questions on the portion(s) of the original sample which brought no response, and thus on those who were selected (or available) for re-interview. Indeed, one could raise a number of technical questions about the unstated criteria for selecting a *'representative'* (yet with a poor response rate) portion of an unscientific sample design (on the basis of final results) in order to 'prove' that the only thing wrong with the sample design was the date on which the final poll was taken. But the ingenuities of what may be called *ad hoc* (sic) *propter hoc* special pleading by each poll would take a good deal of space to do them justice. Needless to say, reputations were saved in 1970, and awkward hypotheses were avoided, such as whether those who replied to re-interview questions did not contain an unusually high proportion of band-waggoners, identifying themselves with the unexpected (by the pollsters and thus, presumably, by the public) Conservative victory. One could ask, again, why the polls did not set themselves the task of discovering whether their original sample designs were faulty. The reply would be, of course, that there could be no means of checking this, since the result of the election was now hindsight, and this in itself would introduce corrupting factors. Yet this argument was not applied to the *re-interviewed* portion of the original sample. Time is ever on the side of the pollsters. All this is not to say that the hypothesis of a late swing in 1970 is disproved. My argument is not that the hypothesis of a late swing is wrong, but that this is not established on the basis of re-interviews any more than the accuracy – or inaccuracy – of other polls is statistically confirmed by those re-interviews.

In a report published in 1972, the Market Research Society concluded that the 1970 Public Opinion Polls had erred because of (a) sampling errors, and/or (b) late swing, and/or (c) bias in the survey methods. The Society was unable to calculate the effects of each or any factor, but recommended interviewing up to the election itself. Clearly there can be no possible objection to such a recommendation, but since the true test of forecasting is to examine a number of forecasts over a period, and not a single, eve-of-election poll, it is by the general run of forecasts that they must be judged.

On this basis the February 1974 election was also a failure for British polls. Again, however, the Market Research Society provided a timely apologia for associated colleagues in polling organisations in a statement of March 1974.[8] The Society's statement began by conceding that the polls had 'confidently predicted' the wrong result. (It is fair to add that it is the press, and not the polls, which reads into the results a good deal of dramatic utterance.) However, the Society's chairman ingeniously 'explains' the false predictions by asking (somewhat rhetorically, as it later appears), 'How far was this a failure of the polls, how much due to misinterpretation of the facts available, and how much due to the electoral system itself?' If, to the culpability of newspaper editors we add the culpability of the electoral system itself, we may be sure that the Market Research Society is beating the bushes somewhat to defend its associates.

The statement proceeds:

> First, the facts. The polls published in the papers on *election day* [my italics: the reader will see the significance] all gave very similar results. The small differences between them were well within the sampling errors associated with these studies. . . . Basically they were all telling much the same story which can be summed up by their average. . . .[9]

Averaging-out is an unusual argument to deploy when precision and particular performance are under review, and the statement omits details of the figures supplying the average. Moreover, the average forecast *on the eve of the election* was a $3\frac{1}{2}$ per cent Conservative lead over Labour. The actual result was 1 per cent Conservative lead over Labour. The question not answered – because not asked – is, what were the errors of the previous forecasts? One could select a number of poll forecasts fairly close to election day showing a marked Conservative lead over Labour. For example, the Harris Poll (Conservatives 40 per cent, Labour 33·5 per cent), NOP (Conservatives 43·4 per cent, Labour 37·8 per cent), ORC (Conservatives 41 per cent, Labour 35 per cent), but to cite them proves nothing either way since there is nothing against which they can legitimately be measured. Measured against each other, they resemble each other, but this may prove that they were equally wrong, and not, as is clearly assumed, equally right. Measured against the actual result on election day, the correct conclusion is that they were equally wrong, *unless* there is first established by independent tests the extent – and the direction – of any *uniform* swings assumed to have occurred during the course of the campaign. As we have argued earlier, however, neither an eve of the election poll, nor re-interview of a selected sub-sample is a sufficient post-facto witness for such a shift or shifts. Special pleading by the Chairman of the Market Research Society is understandable. But playing ducks and drakes with the statistics themselves should not go unchallenged.

A distinction is drawn between polls and surveys, in that the latter allow for different sets of preferences and voluntary expressions of opinion through time, rather than the either/or constraints of simple polling. The most obvious constraint in political opinion polls in Britain is that they take as given the public's acceptance of existing party structures and organisations. How justified are they in this assumption? Without derogating from the arguments above on polling techniques, let the pollsters themselves supply some evidence. In September 1972 a poll by the Opinion Research Centre, published in *The Times*[10] showed that 35 per cent of those polled would support a centre party based on a Lib-Lab alliance, but independent of those two parties. The same poll showed 40 per cent would (at the time of asking) vote for a coalition of Liberals, moderate Labour and moderate Conservatives. In another question, 40 per cent said they would vote Liberal 'if there was a chance of the Liberal Party getting into power'. In other words 40 per cent of voters were found to have no special loyalty or commitment to the present party set-up in Britain. In answer to another question in the poll, only 9 per cent felt 'very strongly' that the present political party system in Britain 'works properly'; 53 per cent felt it does not, 20 per cent were 'Don't know'. Decline in voter turnout in 1974, and sharp decline in turnout at by-elections in the 1975–6 period suggest that another, similar poll is overdue.

My reservations, already expressed, on the detaching of opinions from personal contexts is germane here. There is evidence of an innocent, in no sense intentional alliance between existing party organisations on the one hand, and polling organisations (including academic researchers who follow them) on the other. It is not enough to say that voters are always free to say that they support no particular party or that they 'don't know' which party to support. This imposes on the voter a sort of civic negativism which the average citizen (using the tests of ordinary experience) is reluctant to voice to strangers at the door, who must often appear to represent 'authority', with pencil poised. Again negativism *may* involve detailed discussion, and who wishes to discuss civic duties with strangers at the door? Yet when the question is put in a positive way, that is, of supporting a proposed new party, or a possible re-orientation of the political spectrum – especially towards the moderate centre – the replies clearly take an entirely different course.

Questions put in political opinion polls can be defined as constrained and unconstrained. A constrained question takes the present institutional arrangements as given, and, for the purposes of the poll, ineluctable. (Pollsters are often asked to 'assist' voters towards a particular preference in order to reduce the incidence of 'Don't Knows'.) An unconstrained question inquires whether the individual is satisfied with the alternatives proposed to him by the questionnaire. If he is not so satisfied, the correct, and certainly the 'scientific' procedure, is to desist from questions posed on the opposite assumption. Needless to say, unconstrained questions ought to precede, and not follow constrained questions.

In the history of polling and opinion testing, multitudes of constraining questions have been put to individuals, and although it is not the intention of polling organisations to reduce, still less to eradicate differences of opinion (they would argue that, on the contrary, they explore differences), nevertheless the process of aggregation requires the levelling out of differences in order to present results. This formal and technical aspect of polling encourages and sustains constraining questions, as it also puts a high premium on unconstrained questions, if only because these present special difficulties for purposes of aggregation.

Constraining questions are not confined to polling organisations. They are asked, and have been asked, in a very

large number of academic studies. A specific instance will be
more helpful than generalised comment, and since the topic
has provided a considerable amount of empirical research,
we will take class and class attitudes as a useful case in point.
Class is a vast and complex topic, with a voluminous and
differentiated literature. The British social system has been a
favoured arena for investigation, from Marx and Engels to
the present day, and there is an embarrassment of riches for
choice. For obvious reasons, we will exclude ideological,
polemical, or otherwise politically committed commentaries.
Our choice should properly be made from dispassionate,
empirical studies, free from bias or prior commitment.

For a discussion of class attitudes as these affect political
preferences in Britain, it would be difficult to find a more
carefully researched, balanced and sophisticated investigation than that made by Butler and Stokes in *Political Change in
Britain*.[11] The work is no arid piece of social science
mathematisation, since the authors are concerned
throughout to clothe the skeletal outlines of aggregated data
with the practical expression of *volunteered* comment from
individuals, included in selected samples with a careful eye
for geographical and socio-economic spread. The result is a
social document of the first importance which it would be
difficult to fault either on technical grounds or in terms of
humane discussion.

But definitions of class are notoriously difficult. Butler and
Stokes are in good company in stressing the need to define
class with care and caution – even in a society universally
regarded as more class stratified than most developed
countries.[12] Apart from the familiar technical difficulty of
providing criteria – objective, subjective or a mixture of both,
for defining social class – investigators have repeatedly
encountered a practical difficulty in the reluctance of
individuals to assign themselves to a particular class,
especially at the lower ends of any presumed class ladder.
Thus, in 1964 Butler and Stokes found that, for a randomly
selected half of their sample, only 50 per cent replied 'Yes' to
the question 'Do you ever think of yourself as belonging to a

particular class?' To those who answered 'No', the follow-up question was 'Most people say they belong to either the middle class or the working class. If you had to make a choice, would you call yourself middle class or working class?'[13]

It may seem pedantic to suggest that the follow-up question 'Most people say . . .' was falsified by the results of the answers to the first, or preliminary question, but the fact that the follow-up question brought statements of class identification from 93 per cent of the (earlier) recalcitrant 50 per cent is a tribute either to the persuasiveness of the samplers, or the desire of individuals not to be thought aberrant, or to a combination of both, bearing in mind that the 50 per cent who initially did *not* think of themselves as belonging to a particular social class could speak only as individuals, so that they perforce accepted, trustingly, the illicit assertion in the follow-up question '*Most people* say they belong to either the middle class or to the working class. . . .'[14]

We will examine this against the background of several questions on class asked during the three major samplings carried out by the Butler and Stokes investigators between 1963 and 1966. These are set out in Table 1 (page 70).

In the three questionnaires directed to the samples, half samples and by attentuation sub-samples of the inquiry, a fairly wide range of contingent questions was asked about class awareness, class identification, etc. The overall purpose was, most obviously, to generalise these replies to the population at large. Perhaps the most significant reply was given in the 1966 survey, where 54 per cent of the sample did not think of themselves as belonging to any particular class. In 1964, 50 per cent said likewise. Even with the persuasive suggestiveness of Question 65a in the 1963 sample, 34 per cent were either not prepared to acknowledge that 'Most people' identified with a particular class, or alternatively, were themselves prepared to be considered personally aberrant.

A number of questions arise on the captive assumptions of the initial questions directed to the samples and sub-samples,

Table 1

CLASS CONSCIOUSNESS IN BRITAIN
Data from Butler and Stokes, Political Change in Britain

1963 Questionnaire

Q. 65a There's quite a bit of talk these days about different social classes. Most people say they belong to either the middle class or working class. Do you ever think of yourself as being in one of these classes?

(Yes 66 per cent)   (Noes, Don't Knows not given)

Q. 69 (Only to those accepting a class identification): Some people say they have a lot in common with other people of their own class, but others don't feel this way so much. How about you?

(Yes 55 per cent)   (No 37 per cent)   (Don't Know 8 per cent)

1964 Questionnaire

Q. 69a (Asked of a random half sample). Do you ever think of yourself as belonging to a particular social class?

(Yes 50 per cent)   (Noes, Don't Knows not given)

1966 Questionnaire

Q. 67a Do you ever think of yourself as belonging to a particular social class?

(Yes 46 per cent)   (Noes, Don't Knows not given)

---

but perhaps the prime question is this. If, despite the suggestiveness of the 1963 Questionnaire (Question 65a) there was a fairly sharp attentuation in class identification in the 1964 responses (Question 69a), where the question was put in a much more neutral fashion (so that only 50 per cent of a random half sample accepted a class identification), there was a case for re-phrasing the question on class identification to the whole population in a freshly drawn sample. Clearly, this would have been intolerably expensive of time and effort, and one sympathises with the decision to carry on. But the warning sounded again, even more clearly, in the 1966 Questionnaire, where only 46 per cent accepted a class identification. It is, of course, possible that class identification in Britain waned sharply between 1963 and 1966, though a drop of more than 20 per cent (from 66 per cent to 46 per cent in sub-samples), in only three years suggests a remarkably speedy disintegration of the supposed British class system. Projected forward, this would imply that by 1978 every vestige of class identification in Britain will have evaporated.

The moral is clear enough. One can certainly stratify sections and cohorts of the population by level of income, education, and an array of socio-economic characteristics; but whether, from that data, one can go on to deduce, or whether it is legitimate to invent stratification by class in order to facilitate data handling is more questionable. A poorly educated (which is not to say 'lower class') respondent to a questionnaire may well be disposed to accept suggested categories of class distinctions and class awareness, especially if these are put to him by an articulate investigator. The respondent will normally have the civility to feel that the investigator knows what he is talking about, especially if he arrives armed with persuasive suggestions, purporting to be factual statements (*'Most* people *say* . . .'). A more sceptical and less complaisant reaction to the question 'Do you ever think of yourself as belonging to the middle class or to the working class?' might be:

Insofar as I understand the terms you have in mind, or on your questionnaire, the answer is 'No.' Since I work, I must belong to the 'working' class. If my white collar suggests that I am middle class, I do not accept the term if it implies that any other 'class' of persons is beneath, or alternatively above those who work as I do, whether by hand or brain or both. Others may earn less than I do, others earn considerably more, but that does not transform them into a 'class' in the arcane sense which I suspect – but by all means let us discuss the matter at length – you have in mind. Until we have agreed on our definition of terms, your questions pre-suppose categories I do not acknowledge.

When in 1964 Butler and Stokes discovered that only 50 per cent of a random sample agreed (after prompting) that they 'ever' thought of themselves as belonging to a particular class, the proportion dropping to 46 per cent in 1966, as we have seen, there was a strong case for substituting a question in 1966 on the lines 'fewer and fewer people seem to think of themselves as belonging to a particular class these days . . .' and taking the investigation from there, however parsimonious the results may have proved for the (prior) decision to investigate class identification and class voting in Britain in the mid 1960s. The importation of categories is a necessary part of any investigation of voting patterns, but the investigator ought to have in mind that where beliefs and attitudes are concerned, categories are very often imported impositions, rather than felt sensibilities.[15]

I have remarked elsewhere that categorisation (which has its undoubted uses) is an act of culture and is in turn the reflection of a wider, more pervasive intellectual disposition.[16] It is a disposition which regards classification and measurement as an avenue to truths about societies, as well as the individuals which compose them. Societies are thus visually represented in terms of stratified sedimentary layers, one resting on the other, in the typical boxes and diagrams of social science literature. The question of whether the people contained within the boxes visualise society in this manner (as distinct from the social scientist's disposition, for heuristic purposes, to portray them thus) is not explored.

Sediments and strata belong to rectilinear shapes, cast in vertical and horizontal planes, and social scientists are conditioned by their apprenticeships to see them thus. It would be a more complex, but not necessarily a more unfaithful task, to portray societies in nucleic, rather than in stratified forms, possessing both centripetal and centrifugal forces: that is, forces which tend to hold it together – institutions; language; literature; history; legal norms – and forces which tend to make it fly apart: anomic, irrational anarchic, individual and collective. Such a model would be more complex and we would have to revise our thinking fairly drastically, conditioned as we are by several generations of stratifiers and segmenters. But it would not, for that reason, be less faithful to reality.[17]

Notes to Chapter VII

1. Most of the 'Behavioural' debate occurred in the United States, but I use English spelling here. Among the more notable discussions, see Herbert J. Storing (ed.), *Essays on the Scientific Study of Politics* (New York, 1962); James C. Charlesworth (ed.), *The Limits of Behavioralism in Political Science* (American Academy of Political and Social Science, Philadelphia, 1962); Heinz Eulau, *The Behavioral Persuasion* (New York, 1963); and for historical treatments, Bernard Crick, *The American Science of Politics* (London, 1956); Albert Somit and Joseph Tannenhaus, *The Development of American Political Science, from Burgess to Behavioralism* (Boston, 1967). Edmund Ions, *Political and Social Thought in America, 1870–1970* (London, 1971) pp. 17–19, 201 ff.

2. This view is necessarily tentative and may be geographically confined, but it follows from conversations with colleagues and friends at Princeton, Harvard, Yale, Columbia and Johns Hopkins Universities in 1975.

3. Cf. V. O. Key, *A Primer of Statistics for Political Scientists* (New York, 1959), *passim*. The writer retains a vivid memory of V. O. Key's seminars at Harvard in the 1958/9, 1959/60 academic session, where Key's comments on a paper would often begin with the injunction that data and statistics should support hypotheses, not dictate them, and that it is infinitely easier to read too much into the figures, rather than too little.

4. In the well-known Nuffield College Election Studies in Britain, for instance, the 1966, 1970 and 1974 studies show a progressive cautiousness on the interpretation of polls and public opinion surveys.

5. Paul Lazarsfeld and Neil Henry, *Latent Structure Analysis* (Boston, 1968), Chap. 2.

6. The American débâcle in 1948 was not confined to journalists. See the untimely and unfortunate predictions in Louis H. Bean, *How to Predict Elections* (New York, 1948), especially Chap. 14. A sprightly attack on the pollsters appeared, not surprisingly, in 1949; see Lindsay Rogers, *The Pollsters* (New York, 1949). Since then, the record of American polls has been better, because more cautious, but the inescapable fact remains that it is only possible to check eve-of-election polls for accuracy, not others.

7. The immediate post-mortems of the 1970 polls are printed in Richard Rose, *The Polls and the 1970 Election* (University of Strathclyde, Survey Research Centre, 1970) and summarised in F. Teer and J. D. Spence, *Political Opinion Polls* (London, 1973), pp. 183 ff. These commentators accept the apologies of the polling organisations, though Rose supplies a thoughtful discussion of the problems, pitfalls and limitations of election forecasting, *op. cit.*, pp. 47–66. Richard Hodder-Williams, *Public Opinion Polls and British Politics* (London, 1970), clearly wrote most of his book before the 1970 election, but his Introduction contains a useful commentary on the polls of June 1970 – with the interesting remark that ORC handouts were clearly 'looking for a Conservative victory and their copy slanted accordingly' (p. xiii), though adding that the results of surveys were scrupulously reported. Such 'institutional' effects are too complex to discuss at length here and deserve separate treatment.

8. G. J. Goodhardt (Chairman) *Who Got it Wrong – And by How Much?* – The Market Research Society (London, March 1974).

9. *Ibid.*, p. 1. The implication seems to be that provided a newspaper prints (and pays for) all the available polls, by five or six polling organisations, and then averages out all their returns, it has a reasonable chance of correct prediction.

10. *The Times*, 30 September 1972.

11. D. E. Butler and Donald Stokes, *Political Change in Britain* (London, 1969), and Penguin edn. (London, 1973). References are to the 1969 edn. A new, revised edition appeared in 1975, but changes involved affect the arrangement of chapters, and new commentary on, e.g. the Liberal Party. The basic research design, discussed here, is not affected.

12. *Op. cit.*, Chaps. 4 and 5 especially, but see also sections of Chaps. 6, 7, 9, 11–16, *et passim*.

13. *Ibid.*, pp. 66 and 67, fn., and see also *Appendix* (On Questionnaires) pp. 463–506, esp. pp. 478, 491, 505.
14. Strictly speaking, the questionnaire ought to have alternated middle class/working class with working class/middle class, to randomise the subjective appeals of one or other of the classes to individual respondents.
15. For a much more thoughtful investigation of class awareness – or unawareness – approached from the point of view of the respondent, not the social scientist or doorstep investigator – see Elizabeth Bott, *Family and Social Network* (London, Tavistock, 1957), especially pp. 160–75.
16. See p. 136, *infra*.
17. It would require a good deal more space to discuss and develop the model I suggest here, and I must reserve a full treatment for another occasion. I ought, however, to mention that the kernel of the idea owes much to the discussion of centripetal and centrifugal forces in politics raised by James Bryce in his *Studies in History and Jurisprudence* (2 vols., Oxford, 1901), I: pp. 255 ff.

    Note: Since writing the above I have encountered a recent study by Ghita Ionescu, *Government and New Centres of Power: Centripetal Politics* (London, 1975) – a valuable and stimulating book proposing new forms of mediation in post-industrial societies and systems. The author does not mention Bryce, but the argument represents a fresh approach. My own discussion would include forces normally held to lie outside the sphere of formal 'political' decision making, where Ionescu's does not.

VIII

Cross Culturalists

The study of international relations is now a discipline in its own right. It emerged as a combined development, embracing political science and diplomatic history. The post-1950 period witnessed a gentlemanly tussle between advocates of the 'behavioural scientific' school, and those labelled variously (as in the contemporaneous debate in political science) 'normative', 'classical', 'intuitionist' or less scholarly epithets outside the pages of learned journals. The debate within international relations came to a head in the mid 1960s in a series of exchanges in the journal *World Politics*.[1] Thereafter a lull, or truce, or perhaps (if the distinctive fruits of their separate labours provide the key) an agreement to go their separate ways took place.

If the success of a particular approach to a field of study is measured by the number of books and articles published under its aegis, then the behavioural approach to international relations has, in this strictly quantitative sense, dominated American writing for a period of about twenty years now. In Britain the balance has been, and still is, the other way. In France and West Germany the approach is nearer to the British than to the dominant American mode.

Clearly a detailed summary of the 'state of play' would require a long bibliographical essay to substantiate the point. The reader cannot be expected merely to accept the word of one whose particular interests have involved an extensive scrutiny of the literature on both sides of the Atlantic. But the extent of the behavioural contribution may be gauged by reference to such industrious and many-volumed scholars as Hayward Alker, Jr.; Richard A. Brody; Karl W. Deutsch; Harold Guetskow; Ole R. Holsti; Herbert C. Kelman; Robert C. North; Morton A. Kaplan; James N. Rosenau; Bruce M. Russett; R. J. Rummel; J. D. Singer; R. Tanter; and Oran Young.

The use of quantitative techniques in the study of international affairs has been considerably buttressed in the United States by economists (who, of course, would not necessarily accept a 'behavioural' label), such as Kenneth Boulding and T. C. Schelling, and by the mathematically inclined conflict analysts and theorists. The divide between 'behavioural' and 'anti-behavioural' is not clear cut, but there are distinctive differences of approach between the above writers, and a much smaller group of different persuasion which includes Amitai Etzioni; Z. Brzezinski; Roger Fisher; Stanley Hoffmann (see especially his *The State of War: Essays on the Theory and Practice of International Politics* (New York, London, 1965, reprinted 1968)); Hans Morgenthau; Samuel P. Huntington; Robert Osgood; Richard Ullman; and Kenneth N. Waltz. The late Hannah Arendt belonged conspiciously to this second group.[2]

The European picture is weighted against the behavioural approach in the writings of, *inter alia*, Raymond Aron; Coral Bell; Max Beloff; Alastair Buchan; Hedley Bull; M. D. Donelan; Joseph Frankel; Michael Howard; Lawrence W. Martin; F. S. Northedge; D. C. Watt; and Philip Windsor. The quantitative approach is favoured by Stein Rokkan in his work on cross cultural comparisons, and in similar research at the Universities of Essex and Strathclyde. Again these brief listings are not meant to be all inclusive nor, for that matter, mutually exclusive polarities. I refer to recognisable tendencies and emphases, not to rigid schools of thought.

One principal feature of the behavioural approach has been its search for generalisations across nations and systems. This is a natural corollary to a method which emphasises the importance of data and data gathering, rather than too great a reliance on evaluative, philosophical or 'intuitionist' discussion. The result has been to direct the study of international relations towards the analysis of systems – the so-called 'systemic' approach. An important, even a seminal work in this tradition appeared in 1957 – Morton Kaplan's *System and Process in International Politics*[3] – a work which earned favourable comment within the discipline by its bold theses and a highly technical vocabulary, and which influenced a good deal of the writing on international relations, especially on the American side of the Atlantic, in the decade that followed its publication. Since that study illustrates a great many of what seem to me the fundamental errors and shortcomings of the 'scientific' approach to international relations, but also of the behavioural approaches in wider aspects of political studies, I will comment in some detail.

Kaplan takes as given the notion of an international 'system' – or rather, as he develops his argument, a set of systems. He assumes that this approach is both viable and in accordance with the facts. The underlying (and in my view the fundamental) question of whether anything that can be called a 'system' or set of systems operates in the world community is not taken up, perhaps because Kaplan is primarily interested in systems of action. These are defined thus:

> A system of action is a set of variables so related, in contradistinction to its environment, that describable behavioral regularities characterize the internal relationships of the variables to each other, and the external relationships of the set of individual variables to combinations of external variables.[4]

The most interesting aspect of this definition is that by a combination of technical terms, a tautology is given the appearance of a conceptual framework. It states that a system of action experiences processes of action and interaction, from within and without. A political system, it asserts, consists of things that interact with each other, both internally and by stimulus from without. A tautology has its uses, but for analytical purposes, it does not take us very far.

Kaplan concedes that his definition of a system of action may be faulty, since on these terms 'any set of specified variables may be considered a system. Napoleon, the Columbia River and a dinosaur may be considered a system. However it would be most difficult to find a relationship between the variables, and also that relationship would be uninteresting or useless.'[5]

We will pass over the subjective nature of this limiting formulation (which says more or less that if, *ab initio*, the researcher does not perceive interesting or useful relationships between selected variables, they are therefore uninteresting or useless) and concentrate instead on the clues it provides to a fundamental characteristic of the behavioural approach: that data and variables are necessary, hypotheses contingent appendages. There is a process of instant intellectual feedback by means of which the questions are framed by the available data, rather than a process where questions are posed, hypotheses generated and a *resultant* search for relevant data initiated.

Kaplan proceeds rapidly from his proposed conceptual framework to the analysis of what he sees as six distinct international systems.[6] They are:

(1) the 'balance of power' system
(2) the 'loose bipolar system'
(3) the 'tight bipolar system'
(4) the 'universal system'
(5) the 'hierarchical system' [cast in a 'directive' and 'non-directive' form]
(6) the 'unit veto system'

Kaplan agrees that these are not the only kinds of international systems that can be devised, 'but they seem the most representative'. No evidence supports this large claim. Once again a prior and fundamental question is begged. The author proceeds in two pages to specify six different 'rules' of interaction which (in his view) characterise the first or 'balance of power system'. The second or 'loose bipolar system' is allocated twelve 'rules' of interaction. The 'tight bipolar system' is allocated no firm or specific rules, since it is deemed to be merely an extension of the 'loose bipolar' system. The 'international system' is allocated five rules.

It would delay this discussion inordinately to argue that every one of these invented and imposed 'rules' could be the subject of extensive disagreement on definition of terms, specification or applicability; but they provide the author of the study with a number of further chapters for their application to 'national actors', 'international actors', 'supra-national actors' and 'universal actors'. In terms of behaviour, Kaplan sees a further, fourfold categorisation: an 'actor' may be directive or non-directive, and beyond these broad divisions they may be system dominant or sub-system dominant. Kaplan then proceeds to allocate his six systems – with their four different types of actors, to five different 'patterns of choice'. He thus has $6 \times 4 \times 5$, or 120 possible pattern variables to consider, and whilst it would be otiose to suggest that 120^{120} interrelations thus posited within the general framework are too many for purposes of detailed discussion, the formulation leaves open the question of which among that number should be discussed, which left out, and why. But Kaplan does not in fact enter into any such discussion. He proceeds instead to his hypotheses (Chapter 5).

Nine hypotheses are presented, designed to gauge the stability and integration of the various systems and sub-systems. The first three hypotheses qualify as the simplest, least controversial ones, and may be given:[7]

Hypothesis One: Decision-makers within a decision-making unit consider more significant policy alternatives.

This is surely another tautology. It asserts that top decision makers deal with policy matters: persons lower down the hierarchy do not.

Four supporting sub-hypotheses are subscribed to the main hypothesis, but they are lengthy and do no more than provide variations on the main tautology.

Hypothesis Two: Multiple role functions operate on personality systems in such a fashion that the personality systems perceive the objectives and values of the decision-making units linked by the multiple role functions as more similar than they would if they entered only into single role functions.

It is difficult to penetrate the precise meaning of the hypothesis, but it appears to be saying that if people in positions of authority carry out several different jobs, the system tends to be more closely-knit than if everyone has only one job.

Since the nine hypotheses become progressively longer and more intricate (but no less tautological), further particularised comment will serve little purpose. It will be more profitable to consider some general aspects of Kaplan's study, including its method, its highly technical and opaque vocabulary, and some of the intellectual sources from which it clearly sprang.

We have noted that Kaplan begins with a series of definitions concerning system, sub-system and other entities (of which we have mentioned only a small portion here), in order to produce a typology. In this case the typology was six-fold. There is no particular virtue, and certainly no reason in principle for choosing the number six for the discussion and analysis. Twelve or twenty-four, let us say, would involve a more extensive set of definitions, but might well be more suited to the variety of circumstance, whilst three or less may seem unduly parsimonious. But there is no self-evident or demonstrable case for three, six or thirty-six for the typology. The number six resulted merely from a form of reverse reasoning to suit what the author felt would provide a manageable set of variables.

Kaplan's study thus raises more general points on behavioural science techniques. His six-fold initial classification, his welter of 'rules' assumed to apply to each system, his four-fold typology of 'actors', and five-fold 'patterns of choices', together with the nine major hypotheses, all combined within a highly technical, neologistic vocabulary, amounts in sum to a purely abstract discussion. Examples and evidence – whether historical or contemporary – are minimal, save as sweeping statements – for instance, that NATO is a 'non-hierarchical' bloc, whilst Communist countries are (or were) 'mixed hierarchical bloc actors'.[8] These, and other broad definitions are made in order to accommodate them within the typology; supporting evidence is reduced to the merest contingency. We cannot judge whether the theory fits the facts, since, in terms of the vast number of facts available on such broad and complex themes, the fit, even the relevance of the selected facts, are extremely difficult to appraise. What is clear, however, is that the few facts supplied are made to fit the theory. In no visible sense does the theory fit the facts.

A further point is that methodological obsession in behavioural science often involves an abuse of language. I do not mean by this the dense, opaque verbiage which clouds the discussion throughout this particular book, which would be too easy, but also uncharitable to quote in extenso, and Kaplan has written further books in which he rids himself of a good deal of his 1957 style. I mean rather that terms like 'hypothesis' and 'analysis' are not acceptable for this type of excursion. Kaplan's 'hypotheses' are not empirically testable propositions, but wide-ranging assertions which, where they do not turn out to be tautologies, when simplified or translated, give no indication of the sort of evidence that could confirm, or refute, or even challenge the hypothesis. There is thus no analysis in such a study, as the word analysis is used in the natural sciences, the life sciences or in medical science. Instead, there is mere word-play, a juggling of extrapolations whose essentially *non*-empirical character is concealed within a plethora of typologising and conceptualising.

It may be argued that the 'systemic' approach in international relations has made considerable advances since Kaplan's 1957 study. This is true, in the sense that the mathematical tools and quantitative methods deployed are now a good deal more sophisticated.[9] Drawing on the enormous mass of data available from many national and international organisations (for example the United Nations), the scope for quantitative investigation is almost limitless.

Cross-cultural, 'systemic analysis' has thus become a capacious garment covering all sorts and conditions of inquiry, national and international, ranging from business firms and corporations to nation states, alliances, ententes, treaty-relationships and the extensive field offered by the United Nations Organisation and its Agencies. The vast literature spawned under the label 'systemic analysis' often amounts to little more than the refining of platitudes. A prime example is the tautology which asserts that systems undergoing stress will 'load', or inflict strain on their sub-systems.

If 'system' and 'sub-systems' are loosely defined so as to cover all sorts and conditions of institutions, behavioural scientists are assured of permanent employment, disporting themselves in endless inquiries where the appearance of mathematical rigour in the main body of the study obscures the blending of platitude with subjective presumption in the initial research design, not to mention the inconclusive or trivial nature of the conclusions at the end of the study.

The number of such contributions, in the form of journal articles or as papers in edited volumes, is now so vast in what could be termed the International Relations industry, that the problem is to know where to begin. I have criticised one such contribution – an investigation of American attitudes towards Isolationism – in some detail elsewhere.[10] A clutch of further examples can be found in J. D. Singer, *Quantitative International Politics, Insights and Evidence* (New York, 1967). In this work, Singer and a colleague offer a paper on 'Alliance Aggregation and the Onset of War, 1815–1945'. The authors begin by stating that their hypotheses belong to 'the systemic level of analysis'. In the 41 'wars' they identify in the international system between 1815 and 1945 (where World War II involvement is aggregated together with internal friction in the Italian Papal States lasting only eighteen days in September, 1860), the authors explore two main hypotheses: (1) The more alliance commitments among nations, the more war. (2) The closer to pure bipolarity the system is, the more war it will experience.

As to the first, the authors do not – because they cannot – measure their hypothesis against the counter hypotheses, that but for alliances, more wars would have occurred. As to the second, it seems to me entirely unproven by the authors, though it would require an extended discussion on the authors' definitions of bipolarity; 'the international system'; 'major' or 'central' powers; 'peripheral' powers; 'war', and related definitions of the duration and severity of war; the definition of an alliance; and cut-off time for alliances (the authors choose to ignore alliances formed within three months of a war's occurrence, for reasons of statistical convenience, it seems, and not that alliances have a way of increasing as war threatens). One of the hypotheses of this extensive and well tabulated piece of research is that 'each alliance commitment undertaken by a nation reduces its interaction opportunities [since] the allied nation is now less free to compete with its new allies and less free to co-operate with non-allies.' (*Op. cit.*, p. 285.) This is surely a platitude. The more vital question of what sorts of interaction result from *not* being allied (for example, competition leading to *other* conflicts or even moves towards war) is not explored.

The preoccupation with 'systemic' analysis has served, and been served by, the growth of data banks in the United States and Europe, so that a process of mutual feedback has developed. Data banks require a good deal of resource allocation and initial capital investment, and it is not surprising that they are expected to earn their keep by seeking or accepting most of the data they can house. Where doubts on the usefulness of particular archives or data sets exist, the tendency must be on balance to accept, on the familiar criterion that one never knows when or where it might prove to be useful, so better have a surplus of data than a paucity.

One form of feedback has been the development of cross-cultural comparisons and the use of aggregated data, largely pioneered by Karl Deutsch and associates in the United States, but now in the ascendant in Europe.[11] The viability of cross-cultural comparison depends very largely on an acceptance of the metaphysical proposition that ultimately, everything correlates with everything else. And since technological developments in the communications and information industries around the world are now serving up mountains of data, a persuasive tendency exists in the purely technical sense, even if there were not scholars and technicians anxious to promote or accelerate the tendency.

A useful point of entry in what is now a burgeoning literature is provided by a cross-polity survey, and cross-cultural summary, the fruits of research developed at Yale, Harvard and Stanford Universities between 1959 and 1965.[12] One of the principal authors of the studies states that 'the primary hoped-for value' of a further, projected cross-cultural summary, would be the stimulation and con-struction of 'more general and powerful hypotheses as to (1) the interlinkages among various social, cultural and psychological phenomena in the cross-cultural universe; and (2) the mode of causation, or functional significance of such interlinkages'.[13]

These ambitious aims are assisted by computer print-outs. A preliminary step is to define 'inter-linkage' and especially to delineate the circumstances under which the term may be used, the criteria for applying the concept, and equally, for not applying it. The authors attempt this, but the definitions and criteria accepted by them are all debatable, and could be the subject of extensive discussion among social anthropologists and historians, to go no further. Among the prior questions, for instance, are those of defining a culture, what boundaries are set to particular cultures – geographical, linguistic, social, economic, etc.; the historical period, or dates to be selected for the abstraction of data; and the besetting question of whether, and when, like is compared with unlike.

The authors rely on previous work for defining the four hundred cultures they wish to explore.[14] The source materials used by the authors of the cross-cultural summary are thirty-eight in number. This has no mystical significance other than that of the convenience, availability, and criteria of relevance decided on by the researchers themselves. Since four hundred possible 'cultures' are used in the study, thirty-eight basic sources to explore them strikes one as frugal in the extreme.

When one turns to the basic sources, however, one discovers that nine are merely journal articles; four are unpublished doctoral dissertations; two are unpublished bachelor's theses; four are unpublished codings; the remainder are individual studies of varied character, from monographs to selections from published readings and extracts for undergraduate consumption. That the authors of a Cross-Cultural Summary could base a source book of some 2,800 pages on such a shaky edifice is not merely indicative of the disposition of the particular authors, but of attitudes now clearly ingrained in sections of the scholarly community, in the publishing world, and in the international social science fraternity.

When one turns to other 'world handbooks' of political and social indicators, one finds data on economic performance and demographic characteristics which of course legitmately lend themselves to statistical comparisons. But the same volumes include tabulated series measuring, for instance, 'political performance'. Once more one notes a reluctance, or what may now be an inability to see sharp distinctions between factual demographic material, and evaluative political, philosophical and ethical statements. If a principal mark of scholarship is to make, and then to maintain necessary distinctions, cross-polity surveys and cross-cultural summaries fall considerably short of the mark.

In Charles L. Taylor (*et al.*), *A World Handbook of Political and Social Indicators* (New Haven, 1972), the authors supply no detailed sources for their statistics, and at many points one can only be puzzled at their definition of terms. Thus they tabulate 'Regular Executive Transfers' (of government) for a list of countries for each of the years 1948 to 1967. A regular executive transfer is defined as 'a change in the office of national executive from one leader or ruling group to another that is accomplished *through conventional legal or customary procedures, and unaccompanied by actual or directly threatened physical violence*' [my italics]. Switzerland is allotted one every year from 1948 to 1967, which is unsurprising. But Hungary is allotted one for 1956, Greece four for 1967, the Congo is given three in 1960, three in 1961 and one each for the years 1962 to 1965.

By some other idiosyncratic definition, Rhodesia is credited with two 'Renewals of Executive Tenure' for 1965. This is defined as 'an act that re-establishes or re-confirms the tenure of the incumbent national executive leader or group *through the country's conventional procedures*' [my italics]. What is needed in such a 'World Handbook' is a definition of terms, and the criteria for coding. As it stands, such a text is likely to be dangerously misleading before it is informative.

If these data books remained on library shelves, to become the curiosities of another era, mere monuments to an age of over-production among publishers and conspicuous consumption among social scientists, no great harm would be done. But it is clear that they influence established scholars, who have little need to strive for the appearance of cultural – or rather cross-cultural – breadth in their assertions. In his study *The Problem of Party Government* (1974) Professor Richard Rose states (p. 97) that Britain ranks 76th in the world league for voter participation at election times (1970 figures). His source is the *World Handbook* cited above. Yet the table referred to is a rank order headed by Albania and North Korea, each with 100 per cent voter turnout, followed by the Soviet Union (99·9 per cent), Romania (99·8 per cent) and so on down through the ninety per-centers by way of East Germany, Tunisia, Chad and Dahomey. When one also discovers that the rank order is based on the percentage of the electorate voting, but ignores the figures of voters as percentage of the population (in Paraguay, for instance, well above Britain in the rank order, only 49·2 per cent of the adult population are enfranchised) one can only wonder that an established political scientist should use such a thoroughly misleading statistic. But here, as elsewhere, it is number itself that suspends critical faculties to exert a hypnotic effect, and whereas one might imagine that familiarity with number could breed reservations, or at the very least a healthy scepticism, the reverse often seems to apply. Statistics are harvested for data banks with a generous prodigality, and as the global village serves up a million linkages daily, so the paradox develops: real distinctions are eroded or denied and false distinctions – those of the rank order and the correlation matrix – are procured.

Notes to Chapter VIII

1. The exchanges began with an article by Professor Hedley Bull, 'International Theory: The Case for a Classical Approach', in *World Politics* (April 1966). Rejoinders and discussion came from Professors Morton Kaplan, J. David Singer, Marion J. Levy, *et al.*, in subsequent issues, and in *International Studies Quarterly*. The exchanges have been usefully gathered together in Klaus Knorr and James N. Rosenau (eds.), *Contending Approaches to International Politics* (Princeton, 1969).

2. Needless to say there are omissions from the listings given here, and I mean no disrespect to those not included, any more than I intend the two groups to be regarded as mutually hostile camps. Here, as elsewhere in the academy, scholars of different persuasion feel that they have much to learn from each other, they meet amicably and no doubt hope (though it is not for this writer to say) that their colleagues will come to see the error, or the inadequacy of their ways.

3. (New York, 1957).

4. Kaplan, *op. cit.*, p. 4.

5. *Op. cit.*, p. 4.

6. *Ibid.*, pp. 21 ff.

7. *Ibid.*, pp. 104 ff.

8. *Op. cit.*, pp. 75, 79 ff.

9. Cf. J. David Singer (ed.), *Quantitative International Politics: Insights and Evidence* (New York, 1968), esp. Part 3, 'The Systemic Level'. Also J. N. Rosenau (ed.), *International Politics and Foreign Policy* (New York, 1961); J. N. Rosenau, *The Scientific Study of Foreign Policy* (New York, 1971); K. J. Holsti, *International Politics, A Framework for Analysis* (2nd edn., Englewood Cliffs, 1972); John E. Mueller (ed.), *Approaches to Measurement in International Relations* (New York, 1969).

10. The criticism arises from discussion of an article on quantification in political studies. See Ions, 'Politics and Sociology', *Political Studies*, Vol. XVI, No. 2 (June 1968), pp. 177–91, with rejoinder, Vol. XVII, No. 1 (March 1969), pp. 76–8; and my reply to rejoinder, Vol. XVII, No. 2 (June 1969), pp. 218–21.

11. Cf. K. W. Deutsch *et al., Political Community and the North Atlantic Area* (Princeton, 1957); Deutsch, 'Towards an Inventory of Basic Trends and Patterns in Comparative and International Politics', *American Political Science Review*, 54 (1960), pp. 34–57. Arthur S. Banks and Robert Textor, *A Cross-Polity Survey* (Cambridge, Mass., 1963); Bruce Russett, K. W. Deutsch, *et al., World Handbook of Political and Social Indicators* (New Haven, 1964), and subsequent edns. by Charles L. Taylor, H. R. Alker, *et al.*; Richard L. Merrit and Stein Rokkan, *Comparing Nations – the Use of Data in Cross-National Research* (New Haven, 1966); Stein Rokkan (ed.), *Comparative Research Across Cultures and Nations* (The Hague, 1968).

12. The research, its formulation and the methodology used are described by one of the authors, Robert B. Textor, in his 'Computer summarization of the coded cross-cultural literature', in Stein Rokkan (ed.), *Comparative Research Across Cultures and Nations* (The Hague, 1968).

13. Rokkan, *op. cit.*, p. 54.

14. The four hundred cultures are drawn from an ethnographic sample devised by G. P. Murdock for an ethnographic atlas. See G. P. Murdock 'World Ethnographic Sample', *American Anthropologist*, 59 (1957), pp. 664–87.

IX
Content Analysts

Another off-shoot of the 'behavioural' approach to international relations is content analysis. Here, international transactions, in the form of diplomatic notes, messages, telegrams, speeches, statements, addresses and newspaper articles are analysed word by word, or statement by statement. There are affinities here with a school of literary criticism where aspects of style are explored by analysing the structure of sentences, the character of a writer's stylistic traits, including his vocabulary, the recurrence of particular words, phrases and distinctive approaches to syntax. The topic is a lively one, involving a divide between what Dr. F. R. Leavis termed 'Scientism versus Literarism' in a lecture at Bristol University in 1970. But that discussion lies outside the present brief.

In the study of international relations, content analysis has concentrated on themes associated with the onset of war, crisis diplomacy, and the nature of alliances.[1] Various techniques have been refined during the period of more than twenty years in which the study has developed, and it is fair to note that the investigators have moved considerably beyond the crude assumption that the degree of intensity of a relationship, whether hostile, friendly or indifferent, can be gauged by the quantity of communications flowing between them. On the other hand, even the most sophisticated techniques now in use operate on the assumption that the immense variety of communications passing between decision-makers can be broken down into broad, simple themes or categories, with 'key words' 'tagged' for their incidence, great or small.

The quantity of exchanges, and their numerical occurrence, thus remain integral parts of the method and of its built-in assumptions. If a decision maker – let us say a head of government, or foreign affairs spokesman – in adversary relationship with another government, chooses to remain silent for tactical or strategic reasons, then his 'message' cannot be subjected to content analysis, even though the intention and/or the effects of a calculated silence may be of much greater importance than a lengthy note or message. This most obvious device of international diplomacy can be noted by content analysts, but it can hardly be given a weighted value. In diplomatic matters, then, silence is very often golden, but the carat value of particular silences is difficult to aggregate.

Different refinements of basic method have developed in various centres of research, and we will take what would generally be agreed to be the most sophisticated and advanced methods for purpose of discussion. At Stanford University, content analysis has been developed and refined over a period of more than twenty-five years, and a substantial research effort has been applied to themes such as the outbreak of hostilities in 1914, the Cuban missiles crisis of 1962, and diplomacy during the Cold War period after 1945.[2]

Those who carry out content analysis admit that their researches cover only part of the exchanges in international relations. Unofficial exchanges or contacts, the precise timing of a note or message, and above all secret or indirect communications (via third parties) do not feature in the analysis. The question of whether, in any particular diplomatic or hostile exchange these factors are more important for understanding or interpreting the situation, and beyond this the more general question of whether, over longer periods, the true character of international exchanges can similarly be understood and interpreted by selective and partial content analysis, is a large one.[3] What we can do here is to look more closely at the basic postulates of the method and the assumptions necessarily built-in to those methods.

The most obvious prerequisite of the method is that the contents of documents and exchanges be simplified for purposes of classifying, coding and de-coding. The Stanford method requires that all exchanges be reduced to 'unit statements', each containing (1) a 'perceiver' of the action or effect expressed; (2) the 'actor' whose effect or action is being perceived; (3) a (single) 'target' or recipient of the action or expressed effect; and (4) what is termed a 'descriptive-connective', which may best be described as a shorthand formula for categorising the nature of the action or effect expressed between 'actors'.

Clearly item 4, the 'descriptive-connective' requires a fairly rigid system of simplification and classification if the universe of international exchanges is to be reduced to simple formulae. But the simplification goes beyond this. As the authors of the method themselves stress: 'The cardinal rule in coding and preparing unit-statements for scaling is that no assertion must have more than *one* perceiver, *one* perceived, *one* target and *one* descriptive connective . . .' [authors' italics].[4]

One needs to be neither diplomat nor historian to feel that international exchanges occurring – to take the paradigm case – in situations of crisis presaging war, or the outbreak of hostilities, cannot profitably be characterised in this monocular manner. That the coding and computing stage should proceed from these assumptions to 'chart' the state of hostilities between states or groups of states in rank orders, and from this to rank-order-correlations, is naïvely optimistic.

But the crudities of formulation and method are by no means fully covered by our discussion so far. Coding is a laborious task, necessarily given to junior research workers, graduate students, and sometimes to undergraduates. Built-in checks are applied at regular intervals, so that the coding decisions of one 'judge' are tested against those of another.

In one elaborate piece of research, dealing with American–Soviet exchanges at the time of the Cuban missiles crisis of 1962, a methodological Appendix gives details of a test of the three 'judges' (Stanford University students), and their coding performances at a particular stage. The test showed that the level of agreement between three judges varied from 0·967 to 0·842 ('significant at beyond the 0·01 level'). The methodological Appendix fails to note that comparison of performance between three young American university students (presumably closely acquainted after many coding sessions), undergoing much the same process of education at the same university, can hardly be counted an objective test *of the method or the coding*. It would be surprising indeed if the three young judges did not show a degree of similarity in coding the exchanges between the United States and Russia during the Cuban missiles crisis. The test applied was thus a witness not to the reliability of the coding, nor to the methodology, but to the similar intellectual, ideological and socio-economic characteristics of the 'judges'.

There are other technical aspects of the Stanford Inquirer (to give the system its institutional name) which raise questions, but we will restrict comment to one more. For declared reasons of 'convenience and economy' any given universe of statements (in a particular research topic) is reduced or 'forced', in the researchers' terminology, into a nine category classification. As they put it, this distribution 'is prescribed or forced to help insure that scaling judges will make the necessary fine distinctions'.[6] This produces a 'Q-Sort' scale which is in turn based on the assumption that 'in a representative sample of a given phenomenon, a greater number of units will manifest an "average" or moderate expression of a quality than an extreme expression'. Q-Sort distribution thus approximates to 'normal curve' as this occurs in statistics. This (explicitly) forced symmetrical distribution of the Q-Sort thus rests on the remarkable assumption that in diplomatic crises, exchanges follow 'normal curve' characteristics in the incidence of 'average' or 'moderate' expressions. A further refinement of the scaling method requires 'judges' to allocate statements into the nine categories on a strict quota basis, with a restriction for each category. Thus are the errant processes of diplomacy made neat by subjecting them to the tidy universe of computer packaging.

It may seem more profitable to turn from methodological discussion to the fruits, or at least to the conclusions of these elaborate, labour-intensive exercises in content analysis issuing from research centres specialising in such techniques. But here again there is a difficulty, since the conclusions can neither be established and agreed to, nor discounted on the basis of contrary evidence elsewhere. The most that can issue are verdicts of suspended belief. The researchers establish, by means of an abundance of tables, with rank-order correlations, that greater quantities or lesser quantities of friendly or aversive statements passed between governments in selected periods. Number, therefore, is the governing factor in charting friendly or aversive dispositions. The data establish or appear to establish that greater degrees of friendliness or greater degrees of hostility existed at particular periods. Immense quantities of documents are used to reach these conclusions. A well-known study of the onset of war in 1914 by a leading researcher in the field used 5,269 documents from 1914 in order to produce 4,833 'perceptions' for purposes of coding. The hypotheses for testing in the research were, as the researcher admits, common-sensical. A typical one is Hypothesis 1:

As stress increases in a crisis situation,
   (a) Time will be perceived as an increasingly salient factor in decision-making.
   (b) Decision-makers will become increasingly concerned with the immediate rather than the distant future.[7]

A sophisticated statistical treatment follows the formulation of these hypotheses. To test them, almost 5,000 'perceptions' from the documents of 'decision-makers' were analysed – giving a total of 160 'time-perceptions'. The reader discovers that during a time of mounting crisis, with a major conflagration increasingly prophesied, *time* was seen as an element in the situation by decision-makers in only 160 exchanges, and that it was *un*important – for purposes of statistical investigation – in 4,740 of the 4,900 exchanges examined. This suggests an unusual degree of sang-froid, or of a reluctance to anticipate and prepare for a likely turn of events. An alternative explanation is that although 'time' perceptions (however identified) were not explicitly expressed in the great majority of exchanges, it was nevertheless present as a potent factor in the minds and thinking of heads of state and other decision-makers, though to have admitted this publicly would have risked creating alarm at home, and given hostages to fortune abroad.

This study of the 1914 crisis raises semantic problems on how a crisis is defined *other* than by a mounting awareness that time is not on the side of peaceful negotiation as adversaries confront each other, exchanges become sharper, and war becomes month by month, week by week, and finally day by day, the expected outcome. If these fears or expectations diminish, and diminish markedly, then by definition the 'crisis' situation postulated in the hypotheses diminishes, and 'stress' – also among the postulates – diminishes too.

By using a sophisticated tool for the study of non-parametric statistics, the same study establishes that the governments of the Triple Entente (France, Russia, England) were significantly more conscious of the time factor in the culminating stages of the crisis of 1914 than in the earlier stages. The data – and statistical tools – also suggest that the governments of the Dual Alliance (Germany, Austria-Hungary) were also moving in the direction of greater preoccupation with the time factor, but the data used in this study did not establish a statistically significant difference between *preoccupation* with the time factor in June–July 1914, as against July–August 1914.

Two fairly fundamental questions can be raised about this elaborate, time consuming, and by any standards expensive piece of research. The first is whether the main conclusion

even if true is not trivial, for what general lessons can be drawn
from this extensive exploration of selected contents of
selected messages passing between selected heads of state in a
unique historical crisis? It would be for the authors of these
and other similar studies to inform us.

The second is whether this particular statistical excursion
did indeed establish the conclusions it claims to establish.
One of the more familiar, but hardly subtle devices of
international diplomacy, and especially of crisis diplomacy, is
to affect an unconcern with time at the precise moment when
time is known to be vital. The device is just one of a
constellation of devices – all inter-dependent – for
strengthening one's hand or improving one's position: a
studied unconcern allays fears in some quarters, increases
trepidation in others; it may reassure allies, it may lull the
suspicions of enemies – real or potential. The technique can
achieve these opposite effects simultaneously, and it is of the
essence of diplomacy – and for that matter of crisis
management – to arrange one's messages and exchanges so as
to maximise one's freedom of movement and to increase
one's options, whilst at the same time diminishing the
options of enemies or adversaries.

In international affairs, the mere letter is not always a sure
guide to the informing spirit, and words are not always
reliable pointers to intentions. Nor is frequency of
communication a sure guide to friendly or aversive
relationships. Communications between 'decision-takers' in
nation states may well increase sharply in the period before
an outbreak of hostilities. They are also likely to increase
sharply in a period of *active* détente. The presumption that
communication patterns in international communications
follow normal curve or other frequency distributions
encountered in statistical theory makes the cardinal error of
assuming that tides in the affairs of men are determined by
consistent criteria. Statesmen will wish that this were so. The
immense resources now deployed on content analysis in the
United States might be more profitably applied to a more
demanding, but ultimately more sophisticated exploration of

con*text* analysis, preferably on well grounded historical principles.

Notes to Chapter IX

1. For basic methodological discussions see Bernard Berelson, *Content Analysis in Communication Research* (New York, 1952); Ithiel de Sola Pool, *Symbols of Internationalism* (Stanford, 1951); de Sola Pool (ed.), *Trends in Content Analysis* (Urbana, 1959) and Robert C. North, *et al.*, *Content Analysis, a Handbook with Application for the Study of International Crisis* (Evanston, 1963).

2. Cf. North *et al.*, *Content Analysis* (Evanston, 1963); J. D. Singer, *Quantitative International Politics* (New York, 1967), pp. 123–58; John E. Mueller, *Approaches to Measurement in International Relations* (New York, 1969), pp. 217–47; Dean G. Pruitt and Richard C. Snyder, *Theory and Research on the Causes of War* (Englewood Cliffs, 1969), pp. 62–79; Philip J. Stone, *et al.*, *The General Inquirer: A Computer Approach to Content Analysis* (Cambridge, Mass., 1966).

3. Content analysts often seem unaware that secret diplomacy was the rule until comparatively recently, and that there is still a good deal more vital secret diplomacy (cf. Dr. Henry Kissinger's 'shuttle diplomacy') than open diplomacy. The visits of Colonel Edward House to London in 1916 and his (partly) unrecorded discussions there may (or may not) be much more vital clues to Wilson's decision to enter the war than the formal exchange of notes between the Great Powers. Cf. Edmund Ions, *James Bryce and American Democracy, 1870–1922* (London, 1968) Chap. 21; and Arthur Link's *Biography* of Wilson, Vols. IV and V.

4. North *et al.*, *Content Analysis*, pp. 45–6.

5. Pruitt and Snyder, *op. cit.*, pp. 77–8.

6. North, *op. cit.*, pp. 59 ff.

7. Ole R. Holsti, 'The 1914 Case', *American Political Science Review*, Vol. 59 (June, 1965), pp. 365–79. Reprinted in Mueller, *op. cit.*, pp. 226–47.

X

Cliometricians

In recent years historical studies have featured sharp debates
on the strengths and the limitations of quantitative
techniques. There is, or ought to be, no argument about the
value of gathering historical data for purposes of analysis,
since this forms the basis of the historian's craft. The debate
begins where quantification tends to become an end in itself,
leaving little or no room for what the late Richard Hofstadter
called, in one of his last essays, a 'personal voice' for the
historian.[1]

In a sprightly essay on quantification in history,
'Historians in White Coats', Mr. Richard Cobb made some
useful distinctions on the limitations of mere number in
history.[2] Citing his old master, Georges Lefebvre ('Pour faire
de l'Histoire, il faut savoir compter'), Cobb paid tribute to
Lefebvre's immense industry in annexing 300 pages of tables
to his dissertation on *Les Paysans du Nord*. But Lefebvre was far
too wise and experienced a man to think of quantifying the
human act, Cobb noted, since he was too well aware of
human unaccountability and of the accident factor – both in
individual and collective conduct – to venture along that
road.

The distinction between quantifying historical facts and
quantifying human acts is a crucial one, as I have argued in
earlier chapters. Clearly, human acts – like human beings –
are part of the 'facts' of history. But there are facts and facts;

or, to put it another way, facts can be regarded from a variety of perspectives. From one point of view, a fact is no more than a state of mind. States of mind – individual or collective – are part of the data of history. It is the historian's job to explore, estimate, and assess them, relying on his own judgement to interpret what he discovers. Historians from Herodotus to Namier and Lefebvre have used statistical material to assist their researches. Recent debates on quantification in history thus revolve around the overuse or misapplication of statistical concepts and theories to historical material, and not on the use of quantitative *data*. Here, as elsewhere, questions of degree can become questions of kind.

The debate centres on the activities of the self-styled cliometricians who emerged from the ranks of the American Economic History Association in the 1960s. The most widely noticed work to arrive from the new breed of historians is the two volume study of the economics of slavery in the American South, *Time on the Cross*.[3] The authors claim to have over-turned a number of propositions accepted and incorpora-ted in conventional historiography on the topic. These main propositions are that slave labour was inefficient, that slavery was moribund on the eve of the American Civil War, that slavery caused the economy of the South to stagnate, and that slavery involved harsh material conditions for the life of the typical slave.[4] Fogel and Engerman argue that none of these propositions hold good when the data is thoroughly investigated, and there is no doubt that they have achieved a substantial modification of any views of the opposite persuasion.

The question at issue is whether the views ascribed to other historians are as widely held – or as conventional – as the authors imagine. They admit themselves that part of their major thesis is not original, since many of the points they make – and certainly the interpretations they proffer – were put forward by Gunnar Myrdal in *An American Dilemma* (1944). Locating the focal points of the propositions they seek to dislodge is difficult, since the authors scatter their discussion in different parts of the two volumes.[5] Piecing them together, one discovers that the authors claim that a 'traditional interpretation of the slave economy' held sway from 1865 to 1956. It was, they claim, derived principally from Frederick Law Olmsted's writings in several works on the theme of 'The Cotton Kingdom' first published between 1856 and 1861. Another source was Fanny Kemble's Journal (of a residence on a Georgia plantation), first published in 1863. These, together with Hinton R. Helper's *The Impending Crisis of the South* (1857) and John Elliott Cairnes's *The Slave Power* (1862, revised edn. 1863) are held to have established a view of slavery which held until the cliometricians began the work of reinterpretation in the 1960s.

But no such monolithic view of slavery existed at any time between 1860 and 1960. Professors Fogel and Engerman have sought to demolish myths of their own creation. They have moved mountains of data in order to dislodge a molehill of interpretation. As they themselves reveal at several points in a badly organised book (one has to refer back and forth between the two volumes to follow their trail), any 'traditional' or accepted view of slavery was undergoing substantial revision from the moment that Cairnes modified Olmsted's accounts in 1863. The views that James Ford Rhodes took in his monumental nine-volume *History of the United States* (Volume I, 1893) were not those of John B. McMaster in his eight volumes (Volume I, 1883), since both these historians brought their own judgements to a mass of historical material of which Olmsted's writings and Fanny Kemble's journal were only a portion.

Again, the authors identify a whole school of antebellum Southern history with one historian, Ulrich B. Phillips, who published his *American Negro Slavery* in 1918. Phillips is held to have 'dominated historiographic writing on the antebellum South during the first half of the twentieth century.'[6] But in fact Phillips's views were modified and challenged in a succession of works after 1920, including one or two cited by Fogel and Engerman, such as L. C. Gray's two volumes on the history of agriculture in the South (1933), Charles Sydnor's *Slavery in Mississippi* (1933) and the anthropological works of

Melville Herskovits on the American Negro (1928). Neither in the works they cite nor in those they ignore or neglect[7] do the authors establish that a monolithic view of slavery held between 1918 and the 1960s, least of all a 'Phillips School' which they invent to sustain their attack. What *did* occur was a constant process of investigation, interpretation and re-interpretation, which stretched from the works of W. E. B. du Bois at the turn of the century to Kenneth Stampp's *The Peculiar Institution* (1956).

Fogel and Engerman are the prisoners of their own method much more than those they criticise. Whilst they correctly point out that some of the earlier historians, especially those they derogate as 'vicars of humanism'[8] failed to unearth all of the data presented by the cliometricians, it is arguable that the humanists' touch on economic questions was a good deal more sure than the cliometricians' on social and political issues, if indeed they can claim to show any sureness of touch at all. On this evidence, it seems that amassing data does not necessarily develop historical judgement.

When Fogel and Engerman claim to replace impressionistic and uncertain judgements with their own brand of certainty, therefore, they show just that narrowness of outlook coupled with assertive self-confidence which Clio's art is meant to question. The authors charge that old-fashioned 'humanist' historians were too idle to carry out the necessary measurements on the data, or worse, they were 'insensible to the fact that they were smuggling elaborate behavioural models into their books and articles'. But they did no such thing. The notion of some 'behavioural model' – with or without benefit of quadratic equations and linear regression – is entirely foreign to the so-called 'humanist' historians since the whole spirit of their work is that 'models' of human behaviour are improper fantasies. 'Models' can be left to the more rarified reaches of behavioural science. History's canvas is altogether too broad, its art and artifice altogether too intricate to submit to any one model, however elegant or mathematically consistent, and however many symbols and equations are deployed.

Even if one concedes that cliometrics add an extra dimension to historical studies, one can question the technical devices used, from averaging out on the basis of restricted samples to loose generalisations based on uneven historical material. In their rush to quantify Fogel and Engerman overlook the first task of the apprentice historian – to weigh the trustworthiness of the material they select.[10] But a more fundamental charge against cliometricians of the Fogel and Engerman persuasion is that they burke a principal task of the historian, which is to offer an explanation of the events or circumstances they investigate. The reader is told that the material conditions of slavery were much better, and the average slave much more industrious, more reliable, responsible, intelligent and cultured than traditional 'humanist' historians have portrayed. Does this discovery therefore prompt some corrective to any 'conventional' views of the slave-holder, or of the slave population, or of the relationships between masters and slaves? On this point Fogel and Engerman have nothing to say. Their elaborate equations are as silent as they are internally consistent.

In their colourful, passionate and at times polemical account of the quarrels in the ranks of the Economic History Association (Volume II: Appendix A) Fogel and Engerman talk of 'exasperation' in the cliometric camp when their motives seem to be called into question. It was 'pure romanticism', they suggest, that caused the humanists to blanch before the cliometric evidence that slavery was a vigorous, successful, rapidly growing economic system on the eve of the Civil War. Putting on one side all questions of the reliability of source material – or indeed, conceding it for purpose of argument – Fogel and Engerman miss the main point in their sensitive concern with motives, good or bad. As we suggested above, there has never been a blanket 'traditional' (as they argue) view that slavery was at all times and in all places 'inefficient'. To suggest this, however, one must *first* distinguish the terms efficient and inefficient. The most efficient enterprises in history have been labour camps.

The most efficient use of human resources this century, from one narrowly-defined perspective, was the Nazi concentration camp, since unit costs were close to zero, and when some human inputs were expended (by death) remaining resources were utilized by stripping the corpses of further 'inputs' for the enterprise – gold fillings in teeth, gold rings (though this often required severing fingers) artificial legs, spectacles, and any remaining possessions. One does not imply that cliometricians would ever descend to such taxonomies in selecting or distinguishing the 'efficient' enterprises of history. One merely points out that cliometrics provides no clear distinction between these taxonomies.

It is clear that historical studies will encounter more thrusts from these quarters. A number of volumes is already under way in the series *Quantitative Studies in History* under the aegis of the Mathematical Social Science Board in the United States. No doubt the various works will adopt and adapt, in different degrees, statistical tools according to the material and the dispositions of the authors. In a work already available, the papers show marked differences in the deployment of algebraic formulae for the analysis of the topics.[11] These differences are not explained by the nature of the historical data available, since it is always possible in principle, given sufficient data and potential 'variables', to construct models to which the data can be related. Some historians favour models and equations, others clearly do not, and it is here that the divide between cliometricians and non-cliometricians begins.

Consider, for instance, a detailed statistical study of Massachusetts shipping in the colonial period by Bernard and Lotte Bailyn, completed some years before the cliometricians discovered the tablets of their new-found wisdom.[12] The Bailyns set down in meticulous detail the ownership, residence and comparative investments of shipowners in Boston and New England, in London and the British Isles, and in the West Indies, so far as the data could be found. The compilation provides a valuable comparative picture from which we can deduce a good deal about the relative importance of Boston in relation to the rest of America, London in relation to the rest of the British Isles, and further comparisons and contrasts. But the authors claim to present no more than a 'relation' between investors and home ports of vessels in some tables, or the facts of 'concentration' of ownership in certain ports and areas. The treatment does not suggest any correlation between tonnage per investor and place of residence, or number of people investing and densities of population, or between, say, the religion of individual shipowners and the amounts of cargo handled by their deck hands, although these and many other 'correlations' could be attempted. The authors clearly placed limits to the degree of statistical manipulation the material could withstand.

No such inhibitions restrain another piece of historical investigation available from the rich diversity of writings in the United States. In a study of history teaching in German (East and West Germany) high schools in the period after 1948, as reflected in the textbooks used, Richard L. Merrit investigated possible changes in the outlook of the German people in the present century.[13] This is a vast subject, and the author of the study would obviously not claim to have explored more than a small portion of the theme. Here, however, we are interested in the method adopted and not the precise limits of the inquiry.

Merritt based his investigation on six history texts used in German high schools this century, three from the pre-Nazi period, one from the Nazi period, and the remaining two from the post-1948, divided Germany period – one from East, one from West Germany. Merritt confesses a good many difficulties of definition, classification, and extrapolation in the course of his researches. Since it was impossible to consider coding all the events recorded in the six textbooks, the treatment of a single topic – the 1848 revolution – was chosen. Merritt and his co-workers selected twenty-two 'key aspects' of the revolution, although the criteria for selection are not supplied. The numbers of lines devoted to each, in each book, were tabulated, then ranked (from 'most-discussed' topic to 'least-discussed' topic), and correlation co-efficients established, with scores.

An early discovery, *mirabile dictu*, was that the post-war East German text differed from the other five texts. Another tabulation revealed that the text written in the Weimar Republic was fairly similar to that written and used in post-war West Germany. The main conclusions, or 'substantive findings' of the study are:[14]

(*1*) The history text currently used in the East Berlin's high schools differs significantly in its perspectives from that in use on the Western side of the Brandenburg Gate.

(*2*) The East Berlin text has moved further from traditional German historiography on the question of the 1848]Revolution than has the West Berlin text. . . .

(*3*) Although the text written during the Nazi period also tends to be outside traditional German historiography, it is not similar to the East Berlin text. . . .

(*4*) If there is any single text particularly close to that now used in West Berlin it is the book written . . . during the Weimar era. And yet the statistical data indicate that there is only a suggestion of such a tie. The two books differ in too many regards to say simply that one is the spiritual father of the other . . . The complexity of the various relationships discussed in this paper denies the proposition that the historical perspectives of Weimar and Bonn or West Berlin are identical.[15]

(*5*) . . . the East Berlin text is far more inclined than the West Berlin text to stress groups as initiators of action – except with respect to the state and its agents. . . .

The conclusions of the research are: that students in East and West Berlin are receiving images of their past that differ from one side of the city to the other; that in East Berlin the image 'differs sharply from traditional German scholarship', and that 'the role in everyday life of human groups versus more or less impersonal institutions' receives a different emphasis in the two systems (though the author does not make any explicit distinctions on this point).

The symposium in which this piece of research appears includes comments on the essays, and Professor John Higham adds a critical commentary on the method used, and the conclusions reached. Higham wonders if Merritt could not have reached his conclusions without any formal content analysis at all. Certainly the conclusions are such that to receive them other than as self-evident would be to fly in the face of a mass of evidence which goes considerably beyond the narrow compass selected for this piece of research. It follows indubitably from the structure, organisation and ideology (most obviously in its educational theory and practice) of the system in East Berlin that it would, by definition, depart from 'traditional German historiography' – though it should be said in passing that Merritt gives no satisfactory definition of a supposed base line in his paper.

But the prior question surely concerns the author's confidence that a narrowly defined survey (with an abundance of matrices) of one topic in six textbooks provides more reliable evidence of differences of approach than, say, a critical reading of an *assortment* of sources, together with documents of different texture and provenance which touch on the role, purpose, organisation and function of educational institutions in East Germany and in West Germany. The second approach is no more than the familiar approach of any competent historian – and few good historians would stop short at the brief list of sources suggested here – though one suspects that Professor Merritt would argue that the 'traditional' approach to historical scholarship is 'impressionistic'. Yet a narrowly conceived, single-item investigation in six subjectively selected textbooks is itself based on a highly restrictive set of impressions, which are no less impressions for being placed on punched cards for machine reading.

Professor Merritt, the author of this piece of research, is a political scientist, not a historian; and though social scientists turn to historical investigation with the very best of motives –

anxious to contribute, and presumably anxious to learn – the results are not always happy. This is partly because the attempt often begins with a fundamental misunderstanding of the nature of the historian's task, or mere ignorance of his trade. Thus, in a well-known sociological text, an eminent social scientist states that historians are occupied in establishing if not laws, then 'quasi-laws'. He cites a study by two other social scientists in defining this quest for 'quasi-laws' – that is, laws which can still be valid even if apparent exceptions to them are noted.[16] That historians should be regarded as persons engaged in a search for laws, or even 'quasi-laws', will surprise most historians, but it is a good example of the way in which social scientists can misconceive the nature and purpose of historical inquiry by carrying across from their own discipline preoccupations that have no place in related disciplines.

Here, as elsewhere, the imperialistic, colonising tendencies of behavioural science are evident, and whilst mathematical techniques have been used profitably to illuminate areas of the past, and even to challenge established historical interpretations, the craft of the historian is to know the limitations of quantitative techniques as much as their possibilities. Where quantification runs amok, vocabulary itself is infected, so that terms like 'explanation' and 'interpretation' are replaced by a new vocabulary with heavily favoured terms such as 'operationalising the variables'. Or again, in an *ad hominem* fashion that goes oddly with the generalised claims to scientific objectivity and detachment, the 'traditional' historian's judgements and interpretations, drawing on a wide range of materials – or 'data' – are described as 'impressionistic', 'intuitive', even 'subjective', in order to distinguish them from an approach presumed to be detached.

Detachment is a virtue only within certain limits: if the scholar is completely detached from his materials, then he has no interest in them and thus no judgement. To imply, then, that a scholar's 'involvement' with his materials is a shortcoming, is a fallacy. The scholar who takes rapid flight to mathematisation, with or without benefit of computer, is much more guilty of narrow-minded pedantry than the scholar who insists that his researches must cover a wide variety of materials, many of them resistant to content analysis and coding. Historical interpretation is altogether too rich and too uncertain an activity to fit the procrustean limitations of the punched card.

Notes to Chapter X

1. Richard Hofstadter, *History and Sociology in the United States*, in S. M. Lipset and Richard Hofstadter, *Sociology and History: Methods* (a symposium) (New York, 1968), p. 12.
2. *Times Literary Supplement*, 3 December 1971.
3. Robert W. Fogel and Stanley L. Engerman, *Time On the Cross: The Economics of American Negro Slavery* (2 vols., Boston and London, 1974). Volume II ('Evidence and Methods') begins with an interesting essay (*Appendix A*) which traces the emergence of the cliometricians in the American Economic Association in the mid 1960s.
4. The authors claim to overthrow various other, related propositions but I concentrate on the principal ones here for reasons of space. See Fogel and Engerman *op. cit.*, I: 4–6; II: 169.
5. Chap. 5 of Volume I, and *Appendix C* of Volume II are the most relevant, but see also Volume I, *Prologue* and Volume II, *Appendix A*.
6. Fogel and Engerman, II: 171.
7. Neglected texts include A. C. Cole, *Irrepressible Conflict* (1934); G. H. Barnes, *Anti-Slavery Impulse* (1933); A. F. Tyler, *Freedom's Ferment* (1944); W. H. Stephenson and E. M. Coulter (eds.), *A History of the South* (6 vols., 1948–53); W. J. Cash, *The Mind of the South* (1941).
8. Fogel and Engerman, *op. cit.*, II: 10.
9. See, e.g., their strident and iconoclastic tones at *op. cit.*, I: 263; II: 18–19.
10. Cf. Volume II, *Appendix B.*, especially Table B.1. The chief sources (or 'bodies of data' to use the authors' term), were the manuscript schedules of U.S. censuses of agriculture, population and slaves. The authors do not discuss the handicaps, vicissitudes and distorted – to put it no stronger –

circumstances encountered by the census takers, especially on the material conditions of slavery. Fanny Kemble was a better witness than many a wary, or conscience-ridden plantation owner, and Olmsted's on-the-spot accounts in all their rich variety convey the real nature of the slave economy much more faithfully than the 'official' statistics of the 1850 and 1860 censuses.

11. William O. Aydelotte, Allan G. Bogue and Robert W. Fogel (eds.), *The Dimensions of Quantitative Research in History* (Princeton and London, 1972). Contrast the paper by Lawrence and Jeanne Stone with that of Kramer and Lepper; or that of Charles Tilly with the paper by Fogel and Rutner. Tilly and the Stones draw fruitfully on various types of raw data. Kramer and Lepper, Fogel and Rutner leap nimbly into abstract model-building and equation-solving.

12. Bernard and Lotte Bailyn, *Massachusetts Shipping, 1697–1714: A Statistical Study* (Cambridge, Mass., 1959).

13. Richard L. Merritt, 'Perspectives on History in Divided Germany'. In Melvin Small (ed.), *Public Opinion and Historians* (Detroit, 1970), pp. 139–74.

14. *Op. cit.*, pp. 172–3.

15. One can only ask, whoever suggested that they are, or could be, or might be?

16. Harold Garfinkel, *Studies in Ethnomethodology* (Englewood Cliffs, 1967), pp. 2–3. The author bases his discussion on a Rand Corporation monograph by O. Helmer and N. Rescher, *On the Epistemology of the Inexact Sciences* (Santa Monica, 1958). I have not seen the monograph in question, but it appears to subsume history under the 'inexact sciences'.

XI

Jurimetricians

A legal opinion is a complex intellectual exercise. This is a commonplace, but it bears repetition in the light of what will be discussed here. If it is to meet canons of justice as these are commonly understood, legal opinion or judgement should not be the prisoner of past legal opinions, nor should it simply reflect popular opinion. Nor, again, should it expressly seek to be ahead of its time, whether for modish reasons of anticipating changing fashions, or seeking to overturn previous judgements. Sagacious legal opinion will draw elements from all of these considerations, or some of them in particular cases. As Oliver Wendell Holmes Jr. put it in his book on the common law,

> The life of the law has not been logic: it has been experience. . . . The law embodies the story of a nation's development through many centuries, and it cannot be dealt with as if it contained only the axioms and corollaries of a book of mathematics.[1]

Legal logic is an abstruse subject, in which rules of inference, and the distinctions between deductive argument, inductive argument, and *sound* argument present themselves at the very beginning of the inquiry. The attempt to formulate a legal logic has received greater emphasis in Europe than in Britain, in part for familiar reasons of the empiricist temperament. A work such as Ulrich Klug's *Juristische Logik* (1951) was clearly more appealing to continental tastes than to Anglo-Saxon sensibilities.[2] In Britain, the work of Hart and Honoré captures the essential texture of the British approach.[3]

The spirit of jurisprudence in America is best caught in what is perhaps still the most widely read and influential handbook for aspiring law graduates, Edward H. Levi's *An Introduction to Legal Reasoning* (1948). Levi identifies three steps or stages in the pattern of legal reasoning: first, similarity is seen between cases; next, the rule of law inherent in the first case is announced, and thirdly, the rule of law is made applicable to the second case. In the long run, as Levi puts it, a circular motion can be seen. 'The first stage is the creation of the legal concept which is built up as cases are compared. . . . The second stage is the period when the concept is more or less fixed. . . . The third stage is the breakdown of the concept, as reasoning by example has moved so far ahead as to make it clear that the suggestive influence of the word is no longer desired.'[4]

These preliminary remarks are necessary in order to place the discussion which follows in its proper context. The observations of Holmes in 1881, and the brilliantly economical reasoning of Levi in our own time, not to mention an immense corpus of writing in the United States in the field of jurisprudence, are a better witness to the American contribution than the writings I propose to criticise.

Behavioural scientists in the United States have turned their attention to the analysis of judicial decisions. An important, seminal work appeared in 1959.[5] When a sub-discipline reaches the stage of presenting a fairly substantial set of *Readings* in a text designed for universities and colleges, it is safe to conclude that authors and publishers feel that the sub-discipline has a life of its own.[6]

A number of intellectual streams feed into the study of Jurimetrics, as the main text of the school makes clear. Freudianism provided one of the sources – the wish to reveal, if possible, the underlying motives of judges, to subject them to scrutiny, and discover whether they might not correspond with the judges' other psycho-social characteristics. A more general wish to take the mysterious element out of judicial procedures can also be detected, and nearer our own time, interest in judges as members of interest groups – political, or economic, or mixtures of the two.

These intellectual sources can be detected in a study on the United States Supreme Court (Pritchett, 1948) and an earlier article by the same writer, reporting on work in progress.[7] Pritchett began by noting for the period he had under review (1939–41) the incontrovertible fact that in roughly 150 opinions delivered every term by the Justices, the great majority of opinions were unanimous (about 70 per cent of cases). In a substantial number of cases, however, 'the nine members of the Court are not able to see eye to eye' and reach different opinions. Thus, 'if our thesis is correct, these divisions of opinion grow out of the conscious or unconscious preferences and prejudices of the justices, and an examination of these disagreements should afford an interesting approach to the problem of judicial motivation.'

Now clearly, if we define 'judicial motivation' so narrowly as to pin it to private 'preferences and prejudices', both 'conscious and unconscious', there is no argument. Judges, like professors, merely display their preferences and prejudices in putting pen to paper, or giving oral opinion. The question is whether, and to what degree, there are other explanations of verbal opinions and judgements. It would seem that there are, since, if the explanation of divergence is, indeed, personal and private prejudice, then there is a problem in explaining the unanimous opinions of the Justices which, as Pritchett points out, form the majority of cases. It is not enough to say, as Pritchett does, that in all such cases, 'presumably the facts and the law are so clear that no opportunity is allowed for the autobiographies of the justices to lead them to opposing conclusions', since this begs the main question, which Pritchett needs to answer before he embarks on the complex task of unravelling the

Weltanschauung of the nine justices. Is it true to say that cases coming before the Supreme Court – most of them infinitely complex in their mix of private rights, or corporate rights, against the duly constituted authority of the State, at Federal State and local level – arrive tidily in one of two categories, that is, those where the facts and the law are clear, and those where they are not? If not, then a major premise of the investigation breaks down at the start of the inquiry.

Ignoring this difficulty, Pritchett proceeds to the counting of heads in more than 300 cases. This furnishes tables showing the frequency of dissenting opinions among the individual judges. The tables in turn provide a linear scale, locating a judge's dissenting disposition from a notional point of zero, or nil dissent, from fellow justices. This linear scale supplies Pritchett with a major conclusion which speaks for itself.

> Examination of the table shows that with the justices ranked as they are, every member of the Court is placed next to or between the justice or justices with whom he is most completely identified in agreement, and farthest away from those with whom he has least in common.

Quod erat demonstrandum

Pritchett goes on to identify degrees of dissent on a 'conservative-liberal' formulation of right-left, and not surprisingly, he finds some justices more disposed in one direction than another. The definition of 'conservative' and 'liberal' is put simply as pro-government or anti-government, the former corresponding to liberal, New Deal loyalties, the latter opposed to them. In other dissents, attitudes for or against business, and for or against civil liberties are noted.

The conclusions to Pritchett's work, elaborated further in his later, published study,[8] are that some judges were more liberal than others, and some were more conservative than others. Where there is deviant behaviour on the bench, not in accordance with the scores allocated to the particular justice, explanations are along the lines that a Justice is reacting to the balance of opinion among his peers, or say in the case of Justice Stone's 'right wing' dissents, as charted by Pritchett, that 'he has deviated slightly to the right in his views with the passage of time'.

The fact that there is abundant evidence that older judges are not necessarily more conservative than younger judges (Frankfurter, Brandeis, Holmes, and Cardozo provide examples) and that over the years, many Supreme Court judges have moved towards a more liberal position, hardly fits in with this rescue bid to account for Stone's deviant behaviour.

If the jurimetrician replies that statements about judges moving to a more liberal position must be established by mathematical investigation of the data, the answer is twofold. (1) The best evidence does indeed lie in the biographies of the justices, including most particularly the complete texts of their dissenting opinions. This method is no more than the familiar, orthodox approach of the competent historian. (2) If mathematical investigation is preferred, the first step is to define terms fully and unequivocally – 'Left/Right', 'Conservative/Liberal', 'Pro-government/Anti-government'. Such terms, which are common coin if we are discussing matters at the level of daily journalism, become much more conjectural if the matter in hand is legal opinion, where torts are very often mere epiphenomena in complex arguments reaching into the basis of constitutional law, statute law, even natural law, and their interrelationships, to go no further.

Jurimetricians have scaled new heights of sophistication since the early work of Pritchett, Thurstone, and colleagues. Comparisons and correlations between judicial decisions, the religious affiliation of the judges, and of the general population at large was clearly a topic which could not lie dormant for long.[9] For this investigation, the researcher used secondary sources to determine the stated religion of more than 300 judges. Whether the judges practised their religion, as distinct from declaring it, was not investigated. Protestant religions in America were divided (with no supporting argument for the division) into 'high economic status' (Congregationalist, Episcopalian, Presbyterian, and Unitarian) and 'not so-high economic status' (Baptist, Lutheran, Methodist), so that further correlations and scores could be charted. When the scores for sub-groups were charted, differences between the two groups were found to be very marginal. In most cases the sub-groups totalled fewer than twenty judges. These crudities did not inhibit the investigator from presenting his 'analysis' as percentile scores, with estimations of 'chance' accounting for the differences taken to two decimal places.

In the same study, judgements according to 'ancestral nationality' (as suggested by *Who's Who* entries of paternal and maternal extraction) were compared. It was found that those presumed to be of exclusive or part British ancestry, on these crude indicators, differed only marginally in their judgements from those of other ethnic extractions. Once more then, even if we withhold criticism of the crudities of the research design, the number of questions begged, and the considerable number of assumptions and generalisations smuggled into the 'analysis', the results establish nothing that could not be challenged even on the technical basis of the raw data.

Jurimetricians are now disporting themselves among such mountains of data correlating legal opinions with political and socio-economic variables that a new growth industry is present within the American academy. Models have been constructed for 'the mathematical prediction of judicial behavior', and an extensive portion of the standard text is devoted to this.[10] The models presented belong to the realm of pure speculation, and there is no evidence that any have been, or could be, applied to any particular court or group of judges. Defenders of the models will no doubt argue that it is not intended that they should. This raises questions about their status and utility, but one leaves it to the authors to address themselves to these questions.

The doyen of jurimetricians, Professor Glendon Schubert, does indeed take up the topic of predicting judicial behaviour when he refers to a successful case of prediction by one who could not, by any stretch of the imagination, be termed a behaviouralist.[11] In 1962, eleven days before the decision in a historic Supreme Court case, *Baker* v. *Carr* (369 US 186 (1962)), Professor Fred Rodell predicted the outcome of the decision, down to those justices who would be in the majority, those in a minority. He was correct in his forecasting of a split vote, but not quite exact in the result, putting it at five to four, whereas the vote turned out to be six to two (one justice did not participate). In an article explaining how he came to make his forecast, Rodell recognised that votes of the Supreme Court cannot be *entirely* explained by judicial rules, or constitutional principles, but that a vast complex of personal factors – temperament, background, education, pre-Court career, etc. – help to explain particular decisions by particular justices. His approach, then, had been to 'examine the Justices individually as whole human beings', as he put it, and Rodell went on to give examples, in very brief sketches, of his assessments.[12]

In referring to Rodell's successful forecast, Schubert takes the view that Rodell and the jurimetricians belong in the same camp, since they are in the predicting business too. It would be for Professor Rodell to agree to this assertion, since it is by method, rather than by intent, that the matter should be judged. Schubert goes on to make it clear that judicial behaviouralists would never claim to predict particular decisions in a particular court. Rather, they look for behaviour patterns over a period. In other words, Schubert and his colleagues are concerned to observe *general* trends and patterns. 'These are the uniformities about which judicial behavioralists make predictions, because these are the more meaningful and important kind of predictions to make.'[13] Schubert stresses that the US Supreme Court provides the most interesting forum, since its decisions so often affect public policy.

We await, then, successful predictions of the future trend of decisions by the US Supreme Court. No such general predictions are yet available in a literature which is now approaching its thirtieth anniversary.

Notes to Chapter XI

1. Oliver Wendell Holmes, Jr., *The Common Law* (Boston, 1881); new edn. (ed. by Mark deWolfe Howe), Cambridge, Mass., 1963), p. 5.
2. Cf. Joseph Horovitz, *Law and Logic: A Critical Account of Legal Argument* (Vienna and New York, 1972), pp. 18 ff.
3. H. L. A. Hart, *The Concept of Law* (Oxford, 1961; new edn. 1972). See esp. Chapter III, 'The Variety of Laws'; H. L. A. Hart and A. M. Honoré, *Causation in the Law* (Oxford, 1959). (It is difficult to imagine a German or French treatise containing a chapter headed 'Causation and Common Sense', as in Hart and Honoré, Chap. 2.)
4. Levi, *op. cit.*, pp. 8–9.
5. Glendon Schubert, *Quantitative Analysis of Judicial Behavior* (Glencoe Free Press, 1959; New York, 1960). For earlier work, see L. L. Thurstone and J. W. Degan, *A Factorial Study of the Supreme Court* (Chicago Psychometric Laboratory, 1951), and C. H. Pritchett, *The Roosevelt Court: A Study in Judicial Politics and Values, 1937–1947* (New York, 1948).
6. Glendon Schubert, *Judicial Behavior: A Reader in Theory and Research* (Chicago, 1964). The term 'Jurimetrics' occurs at many points in the literature. From it, I deduce the term 'Jurimetrician'. Schubert has tended to use the term 'Judicial Behavioralist', but this strikes me as a misappropriation of the term 'Judicial'.
7. Pritchett, 'Division of Opinion Among Supreme Court Justices', *American Political Science Review*, 35 (1941), pp. 890–98. Reprinted, in part, in Schubert, *Judicial Behavior: A Reader in Theory and Research*, pp. 319–24. Quotations are from this source.
8. Pritchett, *The Roosevelt Court*.
9. Stuart Nagel, 'The Relationship between the Political and Ethnic Affiliation of Judges and their Decision Making', in Schubert, *Judicial Behavior*, pp. 234–59.
10. Schubert, *op. cit.*, Part V.
11. Fred Rodell, *Nine Men: A Political History of the Supreme Court from 1790 to 1955* (New York, 1955).
12. *Georgia Law Journal*, 50 (1962), pp. 700 ff. Cited in Schubert, *op. cit.*, p. 550.
13. Schubert, *op. cit.*, p. 554.

XII
Ethnomethodologists

The principal theme of previous chapters has been that quantification and mathematisation, which are both necessary and desirable to assist investigation in the social sciences, are often required to assume greater burdens than they can bear. I have also argued that the conclusions drawn are either not substantiated, or are otherwise unwarranted, even when the initial postulates of the methods are conceded. A more muted theme has been that in order to justify or to bolster the professed 'analysis', language itself is abused and new lexicons are introduced to accommodate the terms of the investigation. I turn now from mathematics to behavioural language.

A useful starting point to examine this is the literature spawned by Ethnomethodology. The term is itself a barbarous neologism. Even its inventor and chief practitioner has found it necessary to apologise for it.[1] Together with its academic stablemate, Symbolic Interactionism, Ethnomethodology's vocabulary discloses various legacies, including Parsonian system-building and the search for a general theory of action. Persons and individuals are transformed into 'actors' with allotted 'roles' pursuing 'life goals' or 'short-term goals'. Theatrical and dramaturgical terms abound. Apart from nomenclature, verbal and adjectival utterance, too, are cast into tortuous forms of obscurity, where the precise meaning of the terms cannot be disinterred from the transpositions in which they are lodged.

The most widely-read, seminal text in the field is Harold Garfinkel's *Studies in Ethnomethodology*.[2] In the first four pages postulants get their induction through an awesome process marked as 'The unsatisfied programmatic distinction between and substitutability of objective for indexical expressions'. The discussion which follows posits a distinction between what are termed 'objective' and 'indexical' expressions, and whilst respectable intellectual ancestry is invoked for the distinction – notably Husserl and Russell – the distinction is fanciful, dividing statements into those that 'depend upon the relation of the user to the object with which it is concerned' (indexical expressions, deemed to be 'awkward for formal discourse')[3] and those that are free from such subjective personal taints. The distinction drawn would be a useful one if it corresponded to any distinction which exists and is maintained in practice in ordinary speech, but in fact Garfinkel's bifurcation is a figment; a theoretical abstraction which does not correspond to experience. We do not, in conversation or any other form of ordinary human discourse, proceed by the separation and alternation of these two types of expression. Rather, our discourse is suffused by *many* different *forms* of expression. All of these expressions are in a process of verbal interaction, both practically and symbolically, with a variety of social and personal functions to fulfil, and whilst it may be of limited usefulness to identify certain types of repetitious utterance or verbal formulation, one cannot go on from this to build theories on the presumption that two, or three or even a handful of categories adequately capture or characterise the range of expressions in ordinary language.

Thus, although Ethnomethodology places a strong emphasis on 'practical sociological reasoning'[4] and makes practical actions the main area of inquiry, the attempt to substitute 'objective' for 'indexical' expressions – even with the proviso that this is merely 'programmatic' for particular cases – cancels out any claim to practical reasoning, since the formulation of the programme rests on an unreal, indeed a fictitious theory of language use.

The same difficulty occurs in the attempt to provide a definition, or rather numerous definitions of rationality at the end of Garfinkel's book.[5] Basing the discussion on a paper by Alfred Schutz, 'The Problem of Rationality in the Social World', the author prefers a multiplicity of 'rationalities' to any single definition of rationality. The fourteen types of rationality identified could be regarded as a usefully catholic approach to a complex problem that has claimed valuable attention in some recent papers.[6] But the discussion on 'rationality' turns out to be a mere curtain raiser for a quite separate task: the construction of 'an image of a person as a type of behaviour'.[7] In the ensuing discussion the individual once more appears as an actor who may 'rehearse in imagination' various competing lines of action. This flight to dramaturgical fancy itself eludes rational definition.

Garfinkel recognises that everyday life may be different from scientific theorising, and allows four exceptions to his earlier list of fourteen 'rationalities'. A fairly involved discussion follows, which is not enhanced by a profusion of new technical terms and tortuous syntax. At the end, however, the methodological intention is revealed. Rationalities are no more than data.

> No necessity dictates that a definition of rational action be decided in order to conceive a field of observable events of conduct. . . . *Instead of* the properties of rationality being treated as a methodological principle for interpreting activity, they are to be treated only as empirically problematical material. They would have the status only of data and would have to be accounted for in the same way that the more familiar properties of conduct are accounted for. [Garfinkel's emphasis.][8]

This is a convenient way of getting rid of the problem of rationality and of rational behaviour. There is a resemblance to the economist's attempt to circumscribe rationality as no more than an attempt to maximise gains and minimise losses in market situations, though here there is an initial, and superficial, attempt to be more catholic. Fourteen categories of 'behavioural' characteristics are suggested, but then one invokes only four (no more, no less) for *everyday* life, and this disposes of the problem. Behind this formulation is a behaviouristic conviction which, although it appears *prima facie* to be more sophisticated than the crudities of Watsonian behaviourism in the 1920s,[9] is no less grandiose in its claims to explain away old problems. We will turn to the intellectual foundations of behavioural psychology shortly, after discussing another off-shoot, the work of Erving Goffman. Although the epigoni might deny any connection, Goffman and Garfinkel have a great deal in common when the intellectual underpinning of their work is scrutinised.

In recent years Goffman has emerged as one of the most widely-read sociologists. His prolific writings deal variously with non-verbal communication, face to face encounters, interaction ritual, 'role distancing', and what Goffman has termed 'strategic interaction', on which more hereunder.[10] The general theme is symbolic interactionism.

At first reading, it is tempting to see Goffman's work as a valuable, critical development of role theory – taking it considerably beyond the simple models put forward by Ralph Linton in the 1930s, where individuals were presumed – for theoretical purposes – to have single, or dominant roles in their workplace, whilst minor or subordinate roles at home or at play are reduced to mere contingencies.[11] Goffman's important contribution to role theory has been to demonstrate the importance of 'role distancing' in social interactions: that is, those signs and symbols by means of which the individual shows that he has other roles and is not exclusively shackled to a particular role.

This has been a valuable advance, and Goffman's writings gain depth – as well as a great deal of wit and panache – by the wide range of his observations and the variety of sources he draws on, from specialist journals, unpublished dissertations and technical monographs, to spy thrillers, newspapers,

popular weeklies and the advertising media. But as with
Garfinkel, Goffman does not allow us to escape from the
theatrical metaphors of actor, role, audience and scenario.
The idea of a person is not explored. 'Self' is coterminous
with, and indistinguishable from a series of roles or role-
distancing actions. As Goffman puts it, 'Role, then, is the
basic unit of socialisation. It is through roles that tasks in
society are allocated and arrangements made to enforce their
performance.'[12] The resulting paradigm of social interaction
is competitive, or conflictual, whether we are engaged in
concealing our motives from one another, or covering our
retreat in possible threat situations, or avoiding eye contact,
or deploying other gestures and/or ruses to meet or counter
the challenge of daily encounters.

This perspective on human affairs permeates Goffman's
best-known paper, 'Where the Action Is'.[13] The starting point
of the essay concerns two boys who find a coin and decide that
whoever wins the toss keeps the coin. Goffman borrows game
theory terminology, with its 'plays', 'games', and 'pay-offs'.
The essay adds nothing new to game theory, but concentrates
on dividing a coin-tossing 'play' into temporal phases,
named respectively the 'squaring-off' phase, the
'determination' phase, the 'disclosive' phase, and the final
'settlement' phase. The reader begins to feel that this
mapping-out process is a preliminary to new thinking on
coin-tossing, but apart from the introduction of further
temporal divisions (the 'rate' of play, and the 'session' of play
– the latter complete with sequences of four-phase cycles,
with pauses between each cycle), we learn nothing further
about coin-tossing, except that it differs from ordinary
everyday life in that '. . . outcome is determined and pay-off
awarded all in the same breath of experience'.[14] So far, so
simple.

The essay then moves quickly to reportage of certain types
of human activity, the most common themes being gambling
and different types of criminal activity, including robbery
with violence, and other forms of delinquent behaviour. No
single line of argument is pursued and there are many

digressions, including the world of Ernest Hemingway on one hand, and James Bond on the other. Common to all of the examples, however, is a view of human interaction which takes contest (at best) and violence (at worst) as the parameters of interaction. Goffman is obviously far too intelligent, perceptive and widely read to regard these as norms of human behaviour. But conceding this, it is difficult to see in what way this well-known essay contributes to our understanding of ordinary human behaviour. The essay is bursting with selected examples of behaviour where conflict is the mode, but quite what this exuberant, highly selective essay tells us about the rich variety of human behaviour and interaction is debatable.

This partial and selective account of human behaviour is maintained elsewhere in the Goffman canon. As with Garfinkel, a persistent, indeed a universal theme in Goffman's writings is that in their social relations, people are essentially actors, playing roles and putting on performances.[15] The theatrical metaphor is sometimes replaced by a sporting one, where 'players', 'games' and 'teams' replace 'actors'.[16] Common to both Garfinkel and Goffman is a view of human interaction as essentially a performance, assumed or enlisted by the individual in order to 'score' off opponents, real, potential, or imagined. What is absent is any discussion of such elements of human interaction as compassion, sympathy, charity, or love – to name only a few.[17] A child reared on an exclusive diet of Goffman's writings would have no acquaintance with anything that could be termed a moral universe. Life would consist of actors acting out self-assumed roles, alternating with gamesters permanently taking on, or putting down, opponents by means of various stratagems. A person would be no more than a performance, or a set of performances. There would be no further mysteries to the self – that is to say, none that could not be abstracted or deduced from outward and visible performances.

Goffman and Garfinkel belong essentially to the behavioural school of overt performances. Their drastic and diminishing view of personality seems to me dangerously incomplete. One can concede Goffman's social observations on 'the calculative, gameslike aspects of mutual dealings' without conceding that this is in any sense a complete or even an adequate account of human interaction. A clue to that inadequacy is provided by the titles to three of Goffman's books: *Where The Action Is*; *Strategic Interaction*; and *Interaction Ritual*. Throughout, the discussion centres on observed, 'behavioural' exchanges. Action, then, is the key. Action is being, and being is action. Inaction provides no clues to the individual or to self. A person is a being engaged in a game, or a series of games – no less and no more.

It is here that the affinity with earlier, cruder forms of role theory and behaviourism is much closer than Goffman's apologists recognise. Certainly Goffman takes us beyond Ralph Linton's work in pointing out, for example, that surgeons perform a variety of roles both within and outside their daily occupation. But in place of role-playing, we are merely given role-distancing. The more important and fundamental questions concern not the separating out of segmented roles, but their interplay and fusion within the core of the individual human being. The measurement of outward and visible signs under controlled conditions, such as eye-to-eye contact and/or pupil dilation – the basis of elaborate experiments referred to in Goffman's works[18]– reveal the essential affinity with much cruder forms of behaviourism. This relationship is best treated in a separate chapter, where the discussion can be brought up to date, since Behaviourism (as distinct from Behaviouralism) is now a house of many mansions, where experimentation takes many forms, even though the intellectual underpinnings have a common provenance.

Notes to Chapter XII

1. Harold Garfinkel, 'The Origins of the Term "Ethnomethodology"' (1968). Reprinted in R. Turner (ed.), *Ethnomethodology: Selected Readings* (London, 1974), pp. 15–18.

2. Garfinkel, *Studies in Ethnomethodology* (Englewood Cliffs, 1967).

3. *Ibid.*, p. 5.

4. *Ibid.*, pp. 6 and 7 ff.

5. *Ibid.*, pp. 263 ff.

6. Cf. Bryan R. Wilson (ed.), *Rationality* (Oxford, 1970). The twelve essays contained explore the many different criteria for and definitions of rationality. See especially Steven Lukes' essay 'Some problems about rationality', pp. 194–213.

7. Garfinkel, *op. cit.*, pp. 269 ff.

8. *Ibid.*, p. 282.

9. John B. Watson, *Behaviourism* (1st ed. 1924: revd. ed. 1930: reprinted New York, 1970). (Discussed further in Chap. XIII, below.)

10. Goffman's main essays and papers are contained in: *The Presentation of Self in Everyday Life* (London, 1969); *Where The Action Is: Three Essays* (London, 1969); *Strategic Interaction* (Oxford, 1970); *Encounters* (London, 1973).

11. Ralph Linton, *The Study of Man* (New York, 1936).

12. Goffman, 'Role Distance' in *Where The Action Is: Three Essays* (London, 1969), p. 41.

13. *Ibid.* pp. 107–206. The essay is also printed in Goffman, *Interaction Ritual* (London, 1972), pp. 149–270. The profusion of books in which Goffman's best-known papers appear (repetitively) attest to their instant appeal and to a receptive audience.

14. Goffman, *Where The Action Is* (1969 ed.), p. 113; *Interaction Ritual*, p. 156.

15. Cf. Goffman, *The Presentation of the Self in Everyday Life* (1959, new eds. London, 1971, 1972). 'The perspective employed in this report is that of the theatrical performance; the principles derived are dramaturgical', in Goffman, *Relations in Public* (New York, London, 1971), Preface S. II (p. xii).

16. Goffman, *Strategic Interaction* (1969; new ed. Oxford, 1970). Goffman claims to be applying Game Theory throughout, but the claim is quite unjustified.

17. This is not to say that the multitude of examples in Goffman's work do not feature examples of, e.g., courtesy, deference and other lubricants of social interaction, such as ceremonial and ritual behaviour at, e.g., weddings, funerals, etc. My point is that they occur incidentally and as by-products of the interactions: they are neither defined nor investigated in their own terms, but occur as epiphenomena, incidental or tangential to the basic paradigm.

18. E.g. Goffman, *Strategic Interaction* (Oxford, 1970), p. 27, fn.

XIII

B. F. Skinner's Behaviourism

Opinions differ on the progenitors of modern behaviourist psychology. Some favour Aristotle – with his wide-ranging observations of plants, animals and man, the data assembled and classified at the Lyceum rather as the data-collectors of our own time assemble their findings in data banks, with the difference that modern data banks operate with benefit of computers. Others find the intellectual ancestry of behaviourism in Hobbes's psychologism, or the mechanistic explanation of mind in the writings of the French materialist philosopher La Mettrie in his work *Man the Machine* (1748). What is clear is that these inheritances are less proximate than the formative influence of J. B. Watson.

Watson's behaviourism developed as an extreme reaction to the introspective school associated with Wilhelm Wundt at Leipzig, and E. B. Titchener in the United States. Its initial formation is seen best in Watson's early works, rather than his best known work *Behaviorism*, which appeared first in 1924.[1] It is also indubitable that in his flight from William James and the introspective school of psychology, Watson was attracted to the study of animals and birds, where mentalism and problems such as image, perception, purpose, emotion and above all introspection, could either be ignored or at the very least passed over in order to concentrate on overt behaviour patterns. In what must rank as one of the boldest – and most jejune – statements of intent, Watson defined the task of the behaviourist thus: 'His sole object is to gather facts about behavior – verify his data – subject them both to logic and mathematics (the tools of every scientist).'[2] This flight from introspection, as well as from the purposive school of psychology associated with E. C. Tolman and William McDougall, puts Watson firmly in a tradition of inquiry that passes from Darwin, through E. L. Thorndike to B. F. Skinner today.[3]

Professor Skinner is a much abused scholar, and it is not my purpose to add to the harsh epithets levelled against him by English and American commentators who, it seems to me, read into his work a good deal more than a careful reading of Skinner's works should allow. Since he is a much misunderstood writer, a brief digression may be in order to bring out what seems to me the kernel of what Skinner is asserting, even though he finally fails, in my view, to recognise the limitations of his elaborate experiments.[4]

In the development of his research over the past three decades, Skinner has replaced the old term 'reflexes' with his own preferred term 'operants' – that is, motor responses that are emitted spontaneously, rather than by simple reflex actions, whether muscular, mental or a mixture of both. Skinner reasoned that operants could be conditioned; hence the 'Skinner Box', originally a fairly simple apparatus, but developed by successive experiments into a fairly sophisticated device in which Skinner's chosen subjects – mainly pigeons – are studied in varieties of experiments.

At an early stage in his work Skinner also developed the concept of *reinforcement* – chiefly by means of rewards, contingent on the execution of particular tasks. The familiar example is the pigeon pecking at different coloured discs, in different arrangements, or responding to different signals by sight and sound. These 'contingencies of reinforcement' have provided the core of most of Skinner's experimental work, and needless to say most criticism of Skinner arises at the point of extrapolating from experiments with pigeons to suggestions for social engineering for human societies. These now include a 'technology of behaviour' in which socially approved behaviour patterns can be reinforced by appropriate systems of incentives and rewards. Skinner would insist strongly that his proposals are for *reinforcement*, not coercion, or the implantation of behaviour patterns. This makes him a less Orwellian spectre than his more virulent critics suggest. As a person, indeed, Skinner turns out to be a very mild, extremely civilised scholar, as liable to support his points by a reference to Zeno and Aristotle (using Greek) as a quotation from Diderot or La Rochefoucauld.[5] If Skinner has any personal shortcomings they lie in the direction of too great a faith in the possibilities of social engineering, although this is an area in which a civilised, humane optimism is to be preferred to that negative pessimism which results in inaction, or a sense of hopelessness.

It seems to me that the sources of Skinner's behaviourism lie in American idealism, optimism and self-confidence (in technical measures) rather than naïve Utopianism as some critics have suggested, or inhuman social engineering as others have argued.[6] In support of his claims for arranging contingencies of reinforcement in society Skinner cites an experiment in which forty juvenile offenders – all convicted of serious crimes – participated. In the experiment, conducted by Harold Cohen of the Institute of Behavioral Research at Silver Spring, Maryland, boys were taken from the penal establishment to which they had been committed and placed in a different social environment, where imposed discipline was entirely absent. Every boy was free to do nothing if he so wished. Equally, however, every boy could improve his lot, in the way of better food, better accommodation, television, even a free day away from the school, under a system of points-earning. Points could be earned by doing simple chores, but with greater rewards for learning and giving correct answers to examinations after voluntary study periods.

The results were dramatic. Boys thought to be unteachable developed rapidly – learning to read, write, to do arithmetic, and to acquire verbal and mental skills. In the process, the hostile characteristics always in evidence at penal institutions decreased markedly. Later, in follow-up studies, recidivism was estimated at 25 per cent, instead of the customary 85 per cent. At the end of another year, the figure had gone up to 45 per cent, though normal figures would be nearer to 100 per cent.[7]

Skinner may be allowed a measure of confidence, therefore, or if not confidence, of hope, that by changing an environment and re-arranging the contingencies of reinforcement, some social benefits may result. And it is surely worth adding that some notable advances in criminology and the restoration (rather than the punishment) of delinquents has proceeded by means of what could loosely be called 'social engineering'. In this context, and from these perspectives, the virulence of some of the attacks on Skinner seems excessive. Perhaps the clue lies in the willingness, or the alacrity, with which critics of a philosophical or literary turn of mind see determinism, and thus an implied threat to freedom of the will, in anything that smacks of social engineering, even though education is itself a form of social engineering. Skinner has pointed out that when he questions the 'supposed residual freedom of autonomous man' he is not debating the issue of free will.[8]

A careful reading of *Beyond Freedom and Dignity* acquits Skinner of the charge of thoroughgoing determinism. Nor does the familiar charge that Skinner attempts to replace 'autonomous man' with a conditioned robot stand up to close scrutiny. In the first place Skinner explicitly rejects crude environmentalism. He notes the 'ignominious failure' of successive attempts to produce ideal communities, from Owen's New Harmony to the present.[9] On another topic, the heredity versus environment dispute, he points out that both genetic endowment and environmental circumstances play their part in moulding the individual, that 'neither view can be proved', and that in any case such theories have a limited role to play in discussions of cultural differences (Skinner's main focus of interest in *Beyond Freedom and Dignity*), since any parallels between biological and cultural evolution break down at the point of transmission. 'There is nothing like the chromosome-gene mechanism in the transmission of a cultural practice.'[10]

In Skinner's defence it needs to be reiterated, therefore, that he is inquiring into the possibilities of *re*inforcing (not introducing or enforcing) the *existing* contingencies already present in society. He may be accused of false optimism, but not of unthinking social engineering. Nevertheless Skinner's theories fail to convince, it seems to me, in four crucial respects. Firstly, he asserts that 'autonomous man' – the 'homunculus' or 'inner man' of the traditional language of freedom and dignity – is a mythical being, a convenient, yet self-deluding invention to save ourselves from the terrifying conclusion that we are much less the captains of our souls or masters of our individual destinies than we dare admit or recognise. But then there is no such creature in the language of freedom and dignity, whether our sources are Saint Augustine or Aquinas, the novels of Henry James, or Tolstoy, or Dostoevsky, or Camus, or the writings of philosophers or poets, or neuro-physiologists, or criminologists. Instead, there is a continuing dialogue between proponents of different points of view which stress, to different degrees, areas in which man's behaviour is thought to be partly free, and partly determined, or conditioned.

Secondly, when Skinner argues for a shift in the determination of behaviour from autonomous man to the environment,[11] he seems not to realise that the term 'environment' is meaningless if it does not refer primarily to the persons who make up 'the environment'. Institutions may embody certain principles, social, philosophical, political, economic, etc., but their activities (or even, if the term is preferred, their behavioural characteristics) are no more than the actions of the persons who make up the institution and give it its character.

Thirdly, Skinner's proposals fail to meet the old problem, *Quis Custodes Ipsos Custodiet?* Who are the guardians of the public weal who decide what contingencies will be reinforced, and what discouraged? Who operates the operant conditioning and on what principles? How are the guardians

– perhaps technocrats is nearer the mark – selected and for how long, and under what terms do they hold office? These questions are ancient ones, but they are real, and there are good reasons for holding that their resolution would be a much more vital question in Skinner's new society than in our present one.

A fourth criticism relates to Skinner's experiments on animal behaviour – in Skinner's case, pigeons – and his extrapolations from those experiments. A familiar criticism is that analogues from animal experiments cannot be transposed to human behaviour patterns. I am only partly persuaded by this argument, not least because human behaviour under stress, e.g. overcrowding – does at the least have parallels to the behaviour of animals under similar conditions of stress. More research is needed, it seems to me, before any firm conclusions can be drawn. My fundamental objection is that controlled experiments on pigeons (or any animals) need not tell us anything fundamental about pigeons in an uncontrolled environment. A pigeon, a rat or any animal in captive, laboratory environment may well operate levers, or peck discs to secure food, water, obtain rewards, etc. But the repetition of responses, after initially stumbling on the 'correct' (that is, the required) response does not, in my view, necessarily provide clues to the learning behaviour of animals in uncontrolled environments, where the essential characteristics of stimuli are that they are *not* ordered, nor repetitious, but much more random, unpredictable and thus, very often, misleading.

In their natural habitat, birds, animals and living creatures prey or scavenge; there is an element of risk or uncertainty in every activity. In this context a 'conditioned' – that is, the 'required' – response may be entirely unsuitable. Differentiation of response is the key for coping successfully with the unexpected. The prey turns out to be bigger, or more savage than anticipated (let us say, it is defending its young); the fish dives for cover under a bank; the rabbit or the deer vanishes into the undergrowth; the food turns out to belong to a competitor, bigger or stronger than the scavenger or hunter, so that prudence – not to mention a survival instinct – dictates a retreat, in an orderly or a hasty fashion, depending on local and specific circumstance.

Thus it is the *variety* of responses that characterise ordinary behaviour patterns and accounts for success, not the controlled and ordered, hence predictable, responses of the laboratory. From this point of view, Skinner's concepts of freedom and dignity may begin, like Rousseau's, with a noble vision of man shaking off the chains which shackle him, but they end by overlooking the most essential and fundamental prerequisite of his freedom: a perpetual element of uncertainty in the stimulus, and a necessary element of unpredictability in the response. This is surely, in sum, what freedom is about.

Notes to Chapter XIII

1. Cf. J. B. Watson, *Behavior: Introduction to Comparative Psychology* (New York, 1914), and Watson, *Psychology from the Standpoint of a Behaviorist* (Philadelphia, 1919). Watson's strictures on Wundt and Titchener continue in *Behaviorism* (New York, 1924), pp. 1–5.

2. Watson, *Behaviorism*, p. 6.

3. Cf. E. C. Tolman, *Purposive Behaviour in Animals and Man* (New York, 1932), and Margaret Boden, *Purposive Explanation in Psychology* (London and Cambridge, Mass., 1972). Apart from an impressive, scholarly treatment of McDougall's relationship with behaviouralist psychology, Margaret Boden's study includes a valuable discussion on the intellectual background, and the precursors of Skinner and Watson in the German-American schools.

4. Skinner's work *Beyond Freedom and Dignity* (New York, 1971, London, 1972) brought hostile reviews on both sides of the Atlantic. A critical volume of essays on the book – and on Skinner's *œuvre* more generally – has appeared since: *Beyond the Punitive Society*, edited by Harvey Wheeler (Fund for the Republic, New York, 1973 and London, 1973). My own criticism here differs from those put forward in those essays, some of them extremely harsh in tone, and deriving from different perspectives, but the reader is referred to them for a more extended discussion.

5. In 1971 the British Broadcasting Corporation invited Professor Skinner to expound and defend his theses before an invited audience at the Royal Society in the series 'Controversy'. The conditioning process of earlier hostile reviews had led one to expect something in the nature of an anti-humanistic dogmatist. What materialised was a modest, witty, urbane and unpretentious scholar who dealt patiently with the four selected adversaries who attacked his theories in the televised encounter. But the extraordinary range of Skinner's reading can only be captured by reading his works and noting the humanistic character of his references.

6. Skinner's critics tend to read a great deal into Skinner's excursion into the novel, *Walden Two* (New York City, 1960) to bring charges of utopianism. A better perspective might be to wonder how a Behaviourist could maintain his research programme against a good deal of hostility for many years, against competing claims, and still emerge as a Utopian.

7. One could argue, however, that the very special, controlled environment in which the experiments were carried on could never be attempted in society as a whole. Indeed, there is a sense in which the experiments were carried on in an artificial environment, removed (and immunised) from the contagion of just those social forces that produced the delinquent behaviour in the first place.

8. Skinner, 'Answers for my Critics' in Harvey Wheeler (ed.), *Beyond The Punitive Society* (London, 1973), p. 261.

9. Skinner *Beyond Freedom and Dignity* (London, Pelican ed., 1973), p. 181. Elsewhere, however (p. 153) he makes the point that if utopian ventures, perfectionist societies, even planned economies have failed, we should remember that unplanned and unperfected cultures have failed too. 'A failure is not always a mistake; it may simply be the best one can do under the circumstances. The real mistake is to stop trying.'

10. *Ibid.*, pp. 101, 129.

11. *Beyond Freedom and Dignity*, p. 210.

XIV
Lévi-Strauss and Structuralism

Structuralism has spread its wings extensively in recent years and its programme is now an ambitious one. Linguistics, semiology, literary criticism, anthropology, psychology and psychoanalysis are chief bearers of the Structuralist grail, but bridge-building activities are under way in an attempt to link disciplines in some common framework. Hybrid disciplines – and the term is not necessarily pejorative – are sprouting. Sociolinguistics and psycholinguistics are established fields of inquiry. The *terminus ad quem* is perhaps at a point where biochemistry, neurophysiology and linguistics meet in some joint attempt to unlock the code of the human brain.

In its main growth areas, Structuralism has been and remains essentially a French phenomenon, even though it has attracted the interest – sometimes temporary, sometimes prolonged – of scholars elsewhere. Chomsky in the United States, and Edmund Leach in British social anthropology are among those influenced by Structuralism.[1] But the main thrust has come from, and remains essentially French. If we place on one side the great influence of Roman Jakobson, the Structuralist gallery is dominated by thinkers in the French mould. Ferdinand de Saussure in linguistics, Roland Barthes in semiology, Foucault in the history of ideas, Jean Piaget in psychology, Lacan in psychoanalysis, Bachelard, a transitional figure between the early Freudians and later writers, François Jacob in biology, Althusser in political and social theory, and Claude Lévi-Strauss in anthropology. The pantheon is essentially Gallic.

The common inheritance, and the common factor, I would suggest, is Positivism in the French mould. This is not to say that Structuralists do not engage in empirical work, or fail to display the influences of, say, Pragmatism in psychology or linguistics. But my point can be illustrated by examining the work of Claude Lévi-Strauss. The intellectual influences bearing on Lévi-Strauss have been, as one would expect from a much travelled scholar, extremely catholic. Lévi-Strauss has himself acknowledged his principal debts, including Roman Jakobson and Franz Boaz in America, and the earlier influence of Hegel and Marx within the European tradition of dialectics.[2] From these, and a variety of other thinkers, Lévi-Strauss has taken what he needed and incorporated them into his own schema. Nevertheless, the underlying formative influences belong essentially to the French tradition, the chief ones Rousseau, Comte and Durkheim, if we put on one side the more immediate and self-evident debts to de Saussure, Barthes and Marcel Mauss.

Lévi-Strauss has been at pains to distance himself from Comte, but as with his quarrel with Sartre, there is perhaps a greater affinity (positivism, with regard to Comte, dialectics with regard to Sartre) than Lévi-Strauss recognises, or is disposed to admit.[3] Comte's classifications were prior to, not derivative from, existing societies, unlike those of Durkheim, whom Lévi-Strauss favours as mentor and progenitor. But there is a longer stream of inquiry, going from the materialism of La Mettrie, through Condorcet's quest for mathematical rigour, and Comte's for general laws which come together in Lévi-Strauss's expressed purpose of formulating a *logique concrète* covering all systems, in order to provide 'une structure concrète du cerveau' to uncover the code of the human mind.

Discussions of the eventual purposes of Lévi-Strauss's *œuvre* are apt to be stultifying. Leaving aside questions of intent, I will turn to the least disputable aspect of Lévi-Strauss's work – his preoccupation with classification. In *The*

Savage Mind (p. 9), he remarks 'Classifying, as opposed to not classifying, has a value of its own, whatever form the classification may take.' I have written elsewhere that to classify within the human sciences is itself an act of culture.[4] But Lévi-Strauss invokes (*loc. cit.*) the scientist's dislike of disorder, and the consequent need to seek out regularities, to support this assertion. Whether, and to what degree, and for what purpose one should carry over the scientist's methodological procedures in assembling facts and data to the human sciences, especially to the problems of interpreting the sources of myth, is a familiar bone of contention. But one can certainly question – and challenge – the weight Lévi-Strauss attaches to his quoted source: G. G. Simpson's *Principles of Animal Taxonomy* (New York, 1961, p. 5), as well as the conclusion he appears to draw from the same source. Simpson remarks:

> The whole aim of theoretical science is to carry to the highest possible and conscious degree the perceptual reduction of chaos that began in so lowly and (in all probability) unconscious a way with the origin of life. In specific instances it can well be questioned whether the order so achieved is *an objective characteristic of the phenomena or is an artifact constructed by the scientist* [my italics]. . . . Nevertheless, the most basic postulate of science is that nature itself is orderly . . .[5]

It is clear which portion of Simpson's remarks Lévi-Strauss found congenial, but whichever we select, they impose a heavy teleological burden. The natural scientist never lacks evidence that nature is 'orderly', in one sense, since there is a plethora of source material to support the hypothesis. But we can assemble a vast amount of evidence for the opposite hypothesis, even if Jacques Monod, Lévi-Strauss's compatriot, had not put forward an alternative view. In *Chance and Necessity* Monod argued that evolution is unpredictable, a 'gigantic lottery' in which differentiation develops from a 'vast reservoir of fortuitous variability' –

including something like a billion mutations a day, for the human species alone.[6] Or again, the English marine biologist Sir Alister Hardy now feels that natural selection does not account completely or sufficiently for differentiation of species.[7]

For Lévi-Strauss, however, 'The thought we call primitive is founded on this demand for order. This is equally true of all thought, but it is through the properties common to all thought that we can most easily begin to understand forms of thought which seem very strange to us.'[8] This passage is not, as one might imagine, a curtain raiser for an extended discussion of the need to classify, or its inevitability. On the contrary, it leads directly to the notion of bricolage.[9]

Bricolage has puzzled numerous scholars and commentators. It seems to me that Lévi-Strauss never adequately defines either the concept or the activity, *as a universal characteristic*, whether anterior to history, or as a step from nature to culture. We can no more locate it as a defining characteristic of the homunculus than we can locate binarism as an activity in the neurophysiology of the human brain. Bricolage, like binary opposition, is thus a theoretical device. Bricolage allows Lévi-Strauss to accommodate the awkward activity of art and the artist into a scheme which, all protestations to the contrary, fails to accommodate the artistic impulse, and with it the language of spontaneous, creative activity, from prehistory to the present.[10] From this perspective, Bricolage is a necessary diversion, so that Binarism can be given full rein.

This view is not cancelled by Lévi-Strauss's affirmation at several points in the *Mythologiques*, but especially in the final volume, that the central clues to his work lie with music, and that the architectonic construction of the whole can only be appreciated in terms of an elaborate fugue.[11] Without detracting from Lévi-Strauss's affection for, even his involvement in music, we do well to remember that the subtitle to the magnum opus is 'Introduction to a Science of Mythology'. Nor will it do to imply that music and mathematics are ultimately one, in some sublime music of the spheres. This may be true, but the assertion is itself metaphysical, and is not established by ambitious classificatory schemes, binary oppositions, and advanced algebra, even when these are assisted by the resonant invocation of 'cette grande voix anonyme qui profère un discours venu du fond des âges, issue du tréfonds de l'esprit . . .'

Structuralism, like Parsonian general theory, is an attempt to exorcise the ethnocentric cultural devil. It is a high-minded attempt to escape from the parish-pump relativism of the early functionalists. The revolt against Malinowski, Seligman and Radcliffe-Brown has not been confined to France.[12] On the other hand, what is Structuralism if it is not functionalism writ large? From the point of view of hermeneutics, what is that Structuralism seeks – or claims – to interpret? The logic of history? The World Spirit, or the code to the human mind and with it, final answers to the mind/body problem? Whatever its claims, Structuralism is an attempt to impose order on apparent chaos. It is the opium of the polymath, and the religion of the rationalist sceptic; an attempt to impose a design without the argument from design, or any particular ontology. This attempt surfaces here and there in crucial passages in Lévi-Strauss. In *Structural Anthropology* there is a characteristic interlocution in which, after paying court to de Saussure, he opines:

> In anthropology as in linguistics, therefore, it is not comparison that supports generalization, but the other way around. If, as we believe to be the case, the unconscious activity of the mind consists in imposing forms upon content, and if these forms are fundamentally the same for all minds – ancient and modern, primitive and civilized (as the study of symbolic function, expressed in language, so strikingly indicates), it is necessary and sufficient to grasp the unconscious structure underlying each institution and each custom in order to obtain a principle of interpretation valid for other institutions and

other customs, provided of course that the analysis is carried far enough.[13]

Again the argument is circular. The discussion continues to the familiar synchronic/diachronic bifurcation, the model drawn from linguistics, and Jakobson's work in particular. One does not quarrel with the model if it remains where it belongs – that is, within linguistic studies. But culture is not language, and language is not culture, even though it is difficult to imagine the one without the other. Binary oppositions, like bisociation itself, provide useful heuristics, especially for the modern mind, conditioned as it is by Cartesian dualism, the syllogism, and by logical argument. But the moot question is whether – and if so when – these bisociations existed in the primitive mind. It is not an answer to this to say that they are everywhere – at all times and in all places – and that this demonstrates their universality. Given time, one could just as easily amass the evidence for a monochromatic or polychromatic formulation in the primitive mind.

The characteristic diagram or drawing in Lévi-Strauss's expositions has symmetry – whether in the form of a matrix, a lemma, or a kinship table.[14] The axes are customarily drawn up and down, left and right, suiting the four nodal points of the compass, and the reasons for this are not difficult to seek. As Lévi-Strauss puts it, 'Any classification is superior to chaos, and even a classification at the level of sensible properties is a step towards rational ordering'.[15] Agreed; but if the task is decoding the primitive mind, rational ordering may not be the appropriate first step, however appealing or seductive the process may be to the present heirs of Descartes, Comte or Durkheim.

The first lesson for apprentice anthropologists is of course to jettison ethnocentric modes of thinking. How far can this be carried? In a valuable series of essays on Lévi-Strauss's study of myth, edited by Edmund Leach, Peter Worsley reminds us that in primitive thought, different kinds of classification exist and that a truthful interpretation may require several different kinds of logic.[16] This is too familiar a point for any social anthropologist, but it is crucial for the *logique concrète* hypothesised by Lévi-Strauss, since diversity, not uniformity, *may* provide the key to any underlying code. The point has reverberations for Structuralist theories of language, notably the Chomsky school, but discussion on this is reserved for the next chapter. Here, Worsley's reminder can be placed alongside some admonitions from a neglected anthropologist, A. M. Hocart, whose career was cut short by his death in 1939.[17]

Hocart's unusual intellectual pedigree of Belgian birth, French extraction, a schooling in Guernsey and study of the classics at Oxford no doubt accounted for a very independent mind, but he certainly anticipated the drift of academic tides. 'The curse of human studies has been endless classifications, definitions, and distinctions till almost every single fact has become a category in itself', Hocart declared. 'How can we make any progress in the understanding of cultures, ancient or modern, if we persist in dividing what the people join and in joining what they keep apart?'[18]

Defenders of Lévi-Strauss may argue that the master has little need of instruction from a neglected ethnographer of the 1930s, yet Hocart's essays are tracts for our time even more than for his own. Every classificatory scheme, like every category, has a built-in teleology, representing a particular cultural perspective. Categories and classes are imported and imposed before they are deduced. This does not mean that classification is an empty or abortive procedure in the investigation of societies, groups or individuals. But it *does* mean that alternative categories and classifications always exist in principle; that no scheme is exclusive or axiomatic; and that to imagine otherwise is to make an elementary confusion between the abstract world of mathematics and the concrete web of social circumstance. Classificatory schemes which admit to being partial, incomplete, or otherwise confined will usually be valuable or illuminating. Those which claim to be universal must first establish the argument by which uniformity, not diversity, is presumed to hold the central clue. It is true that the human species shows differentiation to other species to a marked degree. But differences in degree, especially in the context of evolution, are not necessarily differences in kind.

Notes to Chapter XIV

1. Cf. Edmund Leach, *Genesis as Myth, and other Essays* (London, 1970). It should be stressed that Leach's position has moved on and he is not an advocate of Structuralism. Cf. his lucid book on Lévi-Strauss in the *Modern Masters* series (1970) and Leach, *Culture and Communication* (Cambridge, 1976), pp. 4–5, *et passim*.
2. See Lévi-Strauss, *Tristes Tropiques* (Paris, 1955) and Edmund Leach's *Lévi-Strauss* (Fontana, London, 1970), *passim*.
3. On Comte, see Lévi-Strauss, *La Pensée Sauvage*, Chap. 8. On Sartre, *ibid.*, Chap. 9. (The English translation of *La Pensée Sauvage* renders the title as *The Savage Mind*. This seems to me inaccurate and unsatisfactory. I would propose *Untamed Thought*, even *Primitive Thought* as better alternatives, but with this caveat, further references to the English translation take the existing title.)
4. '. . . To classify is to prescribe and also to proscribe, merely by excluding. By what criteria and on what grounds, general or particular, is it decided that a particular case does or does not fit an unproven generalisation? . . .' Ions, review essay on 'The Legacy of Max Weber', in *Political Studies*, XIX, No. 3 (1971), p. 363.
5. *The Savage Mind*, pp. 9–10.
6. Jacques Monod, *Chance and Necessity* (London, 1972), p. 117. It is a minor irony that one of Monod's sources for this stage of his argument is a later work by G. G. Simpson, *The Meaning of Evolution* (New Haven, 1967).
7. Alister Hardy *et al.*, *The Challenge of Chance: Experiments and Speculations* (London, 1973), pp. 16–17, citing his 1949 Address to the British Association.
8. *The Savage Mind*, p. 10.
9. *Ibid.*, pp. 16–33.
10. *Ibid.*, pp. 22–9. Roger Poole discusses bricolage in his *Introduction* to Rodney Needham's second (revised) translation of Lévi-Strauss's *Totemism* (London, Penguin edn., 1969), pp. 50–52, but the discussion still fails, in my view, to convey

precisely the meaning of the term. Needless to say the fault is not Poole's, stil less that of the translator.

11. See *L'Homme Nu* (Mythologiques IV., Paris, 1971, p. 585). 'La mythologie et la musique ont ceci en commun qu'elles conviennent l'auditeur à une union concrète, avec toutefois cette différence qu'au lieu d'un schème codé en sons, le mythe lui propose un schème codé en images.'

   Lévi-Strauss goes on to suggest that musical and linguistic communication presuppose a union of sound and of sense ('du son et du sens'), but adds (p. 585) '. . . mais il est également vrai d'ajouter que les sons et les sens mis en œuvre par la communication musicale sont précisément ceux dont la communication ne se sert pas.' This surely combines circular reasoning with tautology: music is a form of language, but a distinctive language. The two types of communication can be distinguished, but their message, when decoded, is the same. On the other hand, the type of message carried by music is just that sort which ordinary language is not equipped to convey.

12. Perhaps the most notable defection in England was Evans-Pritchard in his Marett lecture at Oxford in 1950, reprinted in his *Essays in Social Anthropology* (London, 1962), pp. 13–28.

13. *Structural Anthropology* (New York, 1963, London, 1968), p. 21.

14. Cf. *The Elementary Structures of Kinship* (English edn., 1967, ed. Rodney Needham), pp. 154, 163, 165, 188, 191 *et passim*; *From Honey to Ashes* (London, 1973), pp. 32, 89, 325 *et passim*.

15. *The Savage Mind*, p. 15.

16. Edmund Leach (ed.), *The Structural Study of Myth and Totemism* (London, 1967), pp. 153–7, and see Edmund Leach's Introduction, esp. pp. xii-xiii. See also the discussions in Bryan R. Wilson (ed.), *Rationality* (Oxford, 1970), especially the papers by Ernest Gellner, Peter Winch, Robin Horton and Martin Hollis.

17. Cf. A. M. Hocart, *The Life-Giving Myth and other Essays* (2nd impression ed. by Rodney Needham; London, 1969).

18. *Op. cit.*, pp. 23, 156, and see the Editor's *Foreword* to the second impression.

XV
Chomsky and Language

There are important parallels in the work of Chomsky and Lévi-Strauss. Both seek to uncover underlying structures with trans-cultural applications – Chomsky in the study of language, Lévi-Strauss in the analysis of myth. For Lévi-Strauss the universal cement is binarism. For Chomsky, 'deep structures' underpin the language instrument. These lie below the surface structures of sentences, and if we inquire more closely into their precise form, and how they operate, we are told that 'relations' – or in the computer language which Chomsky favoured in his earlier work, 'presettings' – are the clues to universality. If we push the inquiry further, Chomsky summons his hypothesis – and it remains a hypothesis – of 'innate ideas' embedded in the mind at birth. As with the '*logique concrète*' of Lévi-Strauss, however, the precise location in time and place of Chomsky's 'innate ideas' is not established.

Chomsky's debts to Descartes are well-known, and he acknowledges them in his writings.[1] But he qualifies classical Cartesianism on the mind/body problem by arguing that today the term 'physical' is more extensive than Descartes realised. In one prime respect, however, Chomsky is faithful to Descartes in arguing that human beings are distinguished from all other species by the language instrument. In a sweeping – and unproven – generalisation Chomsky asserts:

Modern studies of animal communication so far offer no counterevidence to the Cartesian assumption that human language is based on an entirely distinct principle. Each known animal communication system either consists of a fixed number of signals . . . or a fixed number of 'linguistic dimensions'. . . . In neither case is there any significant similarity to human language.[2]

These are bold claims from a scholar with no formal training in ethology and no experimental work to draw on. We cannot deny what Chomsky asserts, but we can argue that his distinction is not valid, since we simply do not know. Ethologists are only at the beginning of their researches, by contrast to the three centuries of research into language that stretches from the grammarians of Port Royal to the technocrats of the Massachusetts Institute of Technology. As yet we know far too little about animal communication systems to accept Chomsky's suggested distinction.

It is of course a necessary part of the case Chomsky develops in order to distance himself from the Bloomfieldian school of linguistics on the one hand, and behaviourists of Skinner's persuasion on the other. The suggestion that Chomsky is more of a behaviourist than he himself recognises has been well rehearsed by Dr. George Steiner and Yorick Wilks. Like Lévi-Strauss's attack on Sartre, Chomsky's repeated assaults on Skinner may owe less to disparity than to propinquity.[3]

Chomsky's generative grammars, like his 'deep structures' are difficult to criticise, for whilst they are deducible from speech patterns, the crucial question of *how* they are generated and when (in the historical and the biological sense), is nowhere satisfactorily answered. In his rejection of old-fashioned phonetics, and his substitution of 'phonological components' in order to construct matrices possessing 'distinctive features' Chomsky prepares the basis for what he regards as a scientific, or at the least a more scientific, study of language than the old-fashioned linguists could claim.

It is here that, all disclaimers to the contrary, Chomsky is very much more akin to the behaviourists than his self-distancing exercises concede. The link is in Chomsky's attempts to bring mathematical precision to the analysis of grammar.[4] The term 'generate' is itself derived from computational usage, as Lyons has pointed out, and Chomsky's dictum that a grammar is 'a device of some sort for producing the sentences of the language under analysis' is more mechanistic than Chomsky or his followers concede. Moreover, although Chomsky has been at pains to distance himself from what one might call the MIT school of computational linguistics, the early influences are visible even in the transmutations Chomsky shows in his later work. Thus whereas in a *Syntactic Structures* (1957) Chomsky can begin with the claim , 'The set of "sentences" of some formalised system of mathematics can be considered a language', by way of introducing his grammatical/ungrammatical division, he modifies but does not jettison the mathematical underpinning in *Aspects of the Theory of Syntax* (1965) in which he develops von Humboldt's view that 'a language is based on a system of rules determining the interpretation of its infinitely many sentences'.[5]

In his work since 1965, Chomsky has concentrated on the problems of mapping the structures derived from his theories of transformational grammar. Mapping, set theory, and the combinatorial techniques deployed in mathematical and computational linguistics fixes the intellectual parentage of Chomskian linguistics in the Massachusetts Institute of Technology more firmly than in the grammarians of Port Royal or of von Humboldt's school, despite the acknowledgments Chomsky accords to Descartes, Cordemoy and Leibniz.[6]

On the question of Chomsky's relationship with behaviourism, my own view is that Chomsky combines behaviourism with metaphysics, and if the combination is unusual, or indeed unique, this is a compliment to a formidable and complex intellect. Chomsky's behaviourism exists in his detachment of sentences from their normal environment in order to put them through the hoops of his own theories, rather as Skinner separates pigeons from their normal habitat in order to make them perform inside the laboratory.[7] Chomsky's mentalist theories, coupled with his argument that language can be explained by fixed rules, place his theories of language nearer to formal logic than to generative grammar or creative language. Language rules – if, indeed, language can be said to have 'rules' in the ordinary meaning of the word – cannot be subjected to rules of consistency, as with propositions in formal logic.[8] The metaphysical element in Chomsky lies in his theory of 'innate ideas' – a theory that is untested and untestable by any acceptable criteria (but let Chomsky establish the point) but which allows Chomsky to rescue his mentalist theories from the empiricists.

Here as elsewhere Chomsky's combination of psycho-linguistics – his 'mentalism' – and more traditional sources of linguistic studies makes it difficult to place him in any particular stream. This is not surprising since highly original and creative minds are *sui generis*, and Chomsky's contribution is in the new directions he has given to linguistics, not in the adaptation or reformulation of traditional approaches. Yet recent attempts to make linguistics almost a branch of formal logic, with inference rules, mechanical derivations, and the familiar algebraic apparatus we meet elsewhere in behavioural science owes much to Chomsky's considerable influence and his attempt to make generative grammar respond to logical treatment. Further attempts in the more 'advanced' schools of linguistics to formalise generative grammar, together with the construction of artificial languages in mathematics and logic by means of recursive function theory, demonstrate once more the colonising instincts of behavioural science when it comes armed with the tools of mathematics. The notion that a language can be constructed artificially yet still appear to the researcher, or to the technician, to deserve the name (as well as the associations) of language as an instrument, is testimony to the degree of penetration behavioural science has now achieved.

There is little doubt that the new computational studies now flourishing will turn up illuminating data and minutiae on language learning and language use. The danger is that in borrowing tools of analysis from the behavioural sciences, the new breed of grammarians will 'factor out' – to borrow a term they would recognise, if not approve – the substantive basis of their own discipline. The study of language could become – as it is already in danger of becoming – a matter of juggling 'base forms', and 'operators' with assembly lines of ergatives and fricatives, using the existing glossary, in order to supply quantifiers within some General Inquirer of a type already proposed.[9]

Notes to Chapter XV

1. Noam Chomsky, *Cartesian Linguistics* (New York, 1966), pp. 3 ff., *et passim*.
2. Chomsky, *Cartesian Linguistics*, pp. 77–8, fn. 8.
3. On the 'Bloomfieldians' see John Lyons, *Chomsky* (London, Fontana, 1970), Chap. 3. Dr. Steiner's quarrel with Chomsky is set out in Steiner's *Extra-Territorial: Papers on Literature and the Language Revolution* (London, 1972), pp. 102–25. Chomsky's attack on Skinner's *Verbal Behavior* (1957) and on *Beyond Freedom and Dignity* (1971) are now available in several collections, in whole or part. See, e.g. J. A. Fodor and J. J. Katz (eds.), *The Structure of Language: Readings in the Philosophy of Language* (Englewood Cliffs, 1964); J. P. B. Allen, *Chomsky, Selected Readings* (London, 1971, 1972). For the attack on *Beyond Freedom and Dignity*, see Noam Chomsky, *For Reasons of State* (London, 1973), Chap. 5.
4. This point is discussed at greater length, and with much more technical competence than I can claim, in Charles F. Hockett, *The State of the Art* (The Hague, 1968), Chap. 5 *et passim*.
5. Chomsky, *Aspects of the Theory of Syntax* (Cambridge, Mass., 1965), pp. v, 15 ff.
6. Chomsky, *Cartesian Linguistics*, pp. 59 ff.
7. Nor is Chomsky entirely free of old-fashioned stimulus-response theories. In his discussion of innate principles in *Cartesian Linguistics* (p. 63) he makes the surprising assertion 'Of course what is latent in the mind in this sense may often require

appropriate external stimulation before it becomes active . . .' If this is not to be taken as a platitude, Chomsky surely needs to explain the precise status of the stimuli. Are they random and extraneous to theory, or do they follow rules – and if so, what rules?

8. Cf. Charles F. Hockett, *The State of the Art* (The Hague, 1968), Chap. 4, Chap. 5, for a more extended discussion of this point.

9. See P. J. Stone, *et al., The General Inquirer: A Computer Approach to Content Analysis* (Cambridge, Mass., 1966).

XVI
Beyond Behaviouralism

During the last hundred years, social scientists have shown a preoccupation with questions of method which at times has seemed almost a neurosis. From the early Schmoller-Menger *Methodenstreit* disputes in economics in the 1870s and 1880s, through Weber's writings in the Werturteilsstreit and more recently the celebrated meetings of the German Sociological Association at Tübingen in 1961 – not to mention a vast literature on both sides of the Atlantic in the years between – something like a heavy industry has developed.[1] I have suggested elsewhere that social science might profit from a benign neglect of these obsessions.[2] It is no part of my purpose to add to these discussions, but in order to depart from them, it becomes necessary to look back to a particular turning point from which, as it seems to me, these obsessions are in large part derived.

Max Weber is commonly taken to be the main spokesman for the discussion on *Verstehen*, but this view discounts the seminal importance of Dilthey's formulation in his 1883 essay on the humanistic sciences, and the development of his theme in later works in 1894, up to a more systematic statement in 1910.[3] Dilthey distinguished *verstehen* (to understand) from *erleben* (to experience), the second a more subjective concept, suitable for conveying – so far as they can be conveyed – emotions, intuitions, and the feelings aroused by, for instance, aesthetic experience. It is not difficult to trace the path leading from Dilthey's original distinction, and the formulation of *verstehen* to the value-free controversy and beyond to the logical positivists and logical empiricists in the early decades of this century.

The prime error of social science, and more particularly of its lusty legatee, behavioural science, has been to develop Dilthey's lemma along a single track – the one which stresses mental abstraction to the neglect of experience. This helps to account for a remarkable transformation in the meaning of the word 'empirical' in our time. By empirical investigation, behavioural scientists usually mean the type of investigation discussed in the essays in this book, using quantitative techniques, by contrast to what is termed 'normative' discussion or investigation. Yet in its proper, historical associations the word 'empirical' means the very opposite of what behavioural scientists assume it to be. The Oxford English Dictionary distinguishes practical, experimental, and *experiental* aspects of the empirical approach from approaches relying on abstract theory, especially scientific theory. It is the *absence* of the scientific element (real or supposed), then, and the presence of practical observation *based on experience* (not conclusions based on the statistical manipulation of aggregated data) which ought to be the distinguishing characteristics of 'empirical' social science.

It will be argued, of course, that since the behavioural scientists are occupied with the recording of behaviour patterns, whether in small group situations or in larger aggregates, then in that sense they are indeed occupied with 'empirical' investigation. But manipulation of data and the statistical investigation of aggregates are not *per se* matters of experience, even though proficiency in the method is a matter of skills developed by and through experience. The distinguishing characteristics of behavioural science, and its strongest claim to respectability, are that the intervention of human or subjective elements such as ordinary experience, or intuition, are reduced to a minimum, where indeed their effects cannot be avoided altogether in the pursuit of objectivity. This does not produce an 'empirical' programme, but one which is the very opposite, in the search for an axiomatic, deductive system free from the contagion of normative discourse. The quest for objective, value-free behavioural science was misconceived at the outset, and has developed along a particular track of the lemma, with results that I have discussed in the preceding chapters. It follows that there is a cardinal difficulty in attempting to describe the behavioural sciences as 'policy sciences', since the first question for policy makers must be whether, and in what way, theories may be applied. Value-free theorists must not be surprised if policy makers find their theories valueless.

In their preoccupation with modelling and categorisation, behavioural scientists have failed to notice that in modern science, the new concern is for qualitative, not quantitative analysis, and the most exciting discoveries in mathematics itself, even, belong here. Professor René Thom's work on cusp catastrophies deals with discontinuity, not linear progression, and to the extent that his theorems may prove valuable in application to areas such as psychology and problems of cognition, René Thom has uttered a valuable caution on any attempt to universalise his theorems or generalise them in the human sciences.

> You cannot hope to carry out global quantitative modelling unless you have some sort of underlying general rule or general law – like a physical law, for example – acting on the system. But in many very complicated systems like those arising in embryology or physiology there is little hope that such underlying quantitative background exists. I myself have strong doubts about the future of quantitative modelling in many disciplines.[4]

As for prediction, Thom adds, 'I do not think that from any mathematical theorem you can predict anything in reality. Reality is something very different from mathematics, and nothing can be done about that.'

René Thom is one of a number of scientists who convey the true mood and purpose of modern science, as distinct from some outdated, essentially nineteenth-century conception. In an important recent article, the American biologist Gunther Stent argued strongly that quantitative evidence is insufficient, since reality as we know it is no more than a projection; our vision of reality has no incontestable existence separate or apart from our own participation in it, since we are inescapably, at all times and in all places, participant observers.[5] One senses the ghost of Bishop Berkeley peering over the biologist's shoulder at some points, but Stent's position is post-Humean, and derives much more from Kant and Popper than from the good Bishop.

Stent's argument is very much in accord with the position Michael Polanyi reached in his later work. Polanyi's final plea was that scholars in all fields should rid themselves of the 'false ideal of objectivity'. He stressed that complete objectivity is a delusion, and in his own writings demonstrated the importance of different kinds of knowledge and different forms of knowing, including tacit knowing, as distinct from hypothetico-deductive approaches to knowledge.[6]

There are intriguing echoes here of an earlier thinker who rejected the simple bifurcation of Cartesian dualism. In his recent essays on Vico, Sir Isaiah Berlin has brought out not merely the importance and relevance of Vico's ideas, but inferentially a forceful commentary on the quantitative methods of modern behavioural science.[7] In rejecting Descartes' insistence on the deductive method in the *Discours*, and its concomitant stress on geometric methods for the exploration of rhetoric and poetry, Vico advanced his own more profound approach to humane studies. The prime postulate was the role of imagination in ordering the past and the present into intelligible forms. For this task, Vico argued, the *a priori* truths of mathematics are of limited utility. Of much greater importance is a sense of history, created by the historical imagination; a conscious and deliberate attempt to explore the feelings, volitions, insights, intuitions of man's knowledge about himself, then to allow these to play upon the human understanding, in all their contradictions, harmonies, and disharmonies. To exclude such reflections by some narrow circumscription of how knowledge arrives (for instance, by an exclusive insistence on deductive methods) is to impoverish the inquiry.

In his treatment of Vico, Berlin shows the limitations of the restrictive bifurcation 'knowing how' and 'knowing that'. There is a quite different order of 'knowing', Berlin points out, and it was Vico's signal contribution to show its importance and vitality:

> It is a knowing founded on memory or imagination. It is not analysable except in terms of itself, nor can it be identified save by examples. . . . This is the sort of knowing which participants in an activity claim to possess against mere observers: the knowledge of the actors, as against that of the audience, of the 'inside' story as opposed to that obtained from some 'outside' vantage point.[8]

This sense of knowing, this path to knowledge about ourselves, is least discoverable by the 'detached' and 'value-free' methods of behavioural science, even though it is arguably the most important for discovering the real – as distinct from the outwardly observed – nature of our engagement with society. In its reliance on aggregation and quantification, behavioural science thus represents a flight from reality, not a journey towards it.

It may be too much to hope that behavioural scientists should assume a much greater degree of modesty about what can be discovered or divulged by means of quantitative methods. Too much capital and too many resources – especially human resources – are now committed to too many programmes. But as new apprentices to the guild assemble data and prepare to subject them to a multiplicity of tests, deploying all the techniques and devices of behavioural science, one could hope that at some stage they might pause, in order to assess what the programme has achieved in more than a quarter of a century since it flowered in the early 1950s.

Having travelled the road with them, so to speak, in the preceding chapters, I have been unable to locate any important new idea, or any new theorem or paradigm, to borrow a somewhat dog-eared term, that throws fresh light on our condition.[9] Least of all does one encounter findings that could be termed 'scientific', if by that we mean theories or theorems which have been firmly established, and which may be applied to groups within society, or generalised to society itself. Quite apart from the purely technical shortcomings discussed in the preceding chapters, attempts to generalise findings to society, or even to larger cohorts within society, meet the cardinal problem that society is itself an abstraction. As von Mises sagaciously observed, 'Society itself is neither a substance nor a power nor an acting being. Only individuals act.'[10]

Behavioural science can be seen as a form of over-development of the social sciences. If the first stage of growth in the social sciences is put, roughly speaking, from the 1880s to the 1930s, one might call this stage the quest for acceptance and respectability. Behavioural science is the legatee of that quest; an attempt to bring a greater degree of scientism to the inquiry. Scientism is deemed to correspond to mathematical rigour. But as I have sought to show here, such claims are a good deal more illusory than the practitioners appear to recognise, and certainly more than they seem ready to concede.

The argument is not that all social scientists should begin to doubt the utility of their contribution. Investigation of the vast mass of data available in modern complex societies is an invaluable and indeed a necessary pursuit, which belongs in an honourable tradition that stretches from Malthus and Adam Smith, through the work of the great humanitarian reformers of the nineteenth century to magisterial studies on such vital subjects as poverty, relative deprivation, and racial discrimination in our own time. The argument begins where quantification becomes an end in itself, a branch of mathematics rather than a humane study seeking to explore and elucidate the gritty circumstances of the human condition.

In the complex web that makes up a society, where

elements of the past mingle with activities of the present and hopes, fears or aspirations for the future, there are vital elements that are resistant, if not impervious to quantification. These include, for example, as I suggested some years ago, the role of myth, ritual, and symbol – to go no further.[11] To overlook or exclude these elements is to impoverish the inquiry, and at an even more fundamental level to misrepresent what we are about. By its postulates and its techniques of inquiry, behavioural science has become not merely trivial, but in an elemental sense anti-social.

Notes to Chapter XVI

1. Among the most recent, cf. Theodor Adorno *et al.*, *The Positivist Dispute in German Sociology* (papers delivered at the Tübingen symposium in 1961, with corrections and rejoinders), transl. by G. Adey and D. Frisby (London, 1976).
2. Edmund Ions, 'The Legacy of Max Weber', in *Political Studies* XIX, No. 3 (1971), pp. 360–63.
3. For a useful discussion of Dilthey's contribution, see Fritz K. Ringer, *The Decline of the German Mandarins, 1890–1933* (Cambridge, Mass., 1969), pp. 315 ff.
4. René Thom: Interview in *Times Higher Educational Supplement*, 5 December 1975, p. 13. (Thom is Professor of Mathematics, Institut des Hautes Etudes Scientifiques, Paris.)
5. Gunther Stent, 'Limits to the Scientific Understanding of Man', *Science*, Vol. 187 (4148), 21 March 1975 (Washington, D.C.).
6. See Michael Polanyi, *Personal Knowledge: Towards a Post-Critical Philosophy* (London, 1958; revised eds. 1962, 1969), especially the sections on Probability, Articulation and the Logic of Affirmation. See also Marjorie Greene (ed.), *Knowing and Being, Essays by Michael Polanyi* (London, 1969), especially Part 3, 'Tacit Knowing', Part 4, 'Life and Mind'. See also Polanyi's 1970 Nuffield Lecture to the Royal Society of Medicine, 'Science and Man', in *Proceedings, Royal Society of Medicine*, Vol. 63 (1970), pp. 969–76.
7. Isaiah Berlin, 'A Note on Vico's Concept of Knowledge', in *Giambattista Vico: An International Symposium*, ed. G. Tagliacozzo *et al.* (Baltimore, Johns Hopkins Press, 1969); Isaiah Berlin, *Vico and Herder: Two Studies in the History of Ideas* (London, 1976).

8. Berlin, 'Vico's Concept of Knowledge', in Tagliacozzo, *op. cit.*, p. 376. And see Berlin's summary of Vico's approach in *Vico and Herder*, xvi–xix.

9. T. H. Kuhn canvassed the now familiar 'paradigm' concept in *The Structure of Scientific Revolutions* (1962). The term is a useful piece of shorthand, though it does not strike me that Kuhn's thesis, on how science advances, is established. There is useful discussion of it in Imre Lakatos and Alan Musgrave, *Criticism and the Growth of Knowledge* (Cambridge, 1970), especially the papers by Lakatos and Margaret Masterman. Kuhn defends himself in the concluding paper. He also adds a postscript to the new edition of his work (Chicago, 1970), pp. 174–210, where he modifies his earlier position on paradigm shifts.

10. Ludwig von Mises, *The Ultimate Foundations of Economic Science* (New York, 1962), p. 78.

11. Edmund Ions, 'Politics and Sociology', *Political Studies*, XVI (2), June 1968, pp. 177–91.

Index